Quick Weeknight Meals

The Illustrated Kitchen Library

Quick Weeknight Meals

The Illustrated Kitchen Library

Irma S. Rombauer, Marion Rombauer Becker & Ethan Becker

TIME-LIFE BOOKS, ALEXANDRIA, VIRGINIA

Contents

CHICKEN & TURKEY 60

MEATS 80

DESSERTS 104

Introduction

Everybody wants to have food that tastes good, and, especially on busy weeknights, have it fast. Quick cooking from scratch means more than just eat and run. It is a way to spend as much or as little time as you want to treat yourself and those you care for to delicious, wholesome meals on a regular basis. It can be faster, healthier, and less expensive than picking up the phone and calling for pizza or Chinese takeout.

In Quick Weeknight Meals you will find complete meals and quick desserts to top them off. None of the recipes relies on so-called "convenience" ingredients such as taco seasoning and bouillon cubes, which sacrifice taste to save time and usually contain preservatives and artificial flavoring. And each satisfying meal can be on the table in an hour or less, usually much less.

The Streamlined Approach

Quick cooking requires a new, creative approach to how and what to cook. It depends on planning and shopping ahead and keeping often-used ingredients on hand. Having a supply of staples and seasonings at the ready enables you to swing into action the moment you enter the kitchen.

Lacking the benefits of slow cooking—mainly the development of rich and complex flavors—quick cooking requires finding other ways to make foods appetizing. Some tried-and-true methods include starting with flavorful ingredients, for example, basmati or jasmine rice, which are naturally perfumed, instead of plain long-grain rice, as in Lentil and Rice Pilaf with Toasted Cumin Seeds (page 43) and Thai Coconut Rice (page 19). Another way is to use lots of vegetables. Truly fresh vegetables are extraordinarily flavorful and seldom take much longer to prepare than frozen or canned ones.

Bold seasonings, both traditional ones like fresh or dried herbs, spices, and wine as well as less conventional ones, such as Asian ingredients, also make quick-cooked foods taste good. Several recipes call for rice vinegar, sesame oil, chili paste, and fermented black beans. And soy sauce, which, of course, was incorporated into American cooking years ago. Mediterranean ingredients— olives, capers, and anchovies as well as hot chili peppers and herbs like fresh basil and dried oregano—perk up simple preparations of chicken and pasta.

Sun-dried tomatoes and dried mushrooms appear frequently in these quick dishes. Drying fruits and vegetables intensifies their taste, introducing yet another layer of flavor into swiftly cooked dishes. Try combining dried mushrooms with fresh button mushrooms, as in Mushroom Ragout (page 41), which pairs beautifully with polenta (page 41), a comforting grain dish.

Pasta, with its virtually limitless range of shapes and textures and its immense versatility, is a natural for quick meals. All the pasta sauces in Quick Weeknight Meals, whether based on tomatoes, herbs, or mushrooms (pages 30 to 39), can be prepared in the time it takes to cook the pasta.

Kitchen Staples

- All-purpose flour
- Baking powder
- Baking soda
- Breadcrumbs
- Brown sugar
- Cheese: Cheddar, Monterey Jack, Parmesan, and Swiss (refrigerate)
- Cornmeal
- Cornstarch
- Evaporated milk
- Nuts: almonds, peanuts, pistachios, and walnuts (freeze)
- Oil: corn, olive, and peanut oil
- Raisins
- Red pepper flakes
- Tomatoes, canned
- Tomatoes, sun-dried
- Tomato paste
- Tomato sauce
- Vinegar: rice wine, sherry, and wine vinegar

Techniques That Reward

Employing up-to-date cooking tricks like scorching onions, as in Pan-Seared Top Round Steak with Smoky Onions and Red Wine (page 83), or caramelizing them to bring out their sweet taste contributes subtle nuances to a finished dish. Starting a sauce by frying onion, carrots, and garlic in oil, as in Maria's Twenty-Minute Tomato Sauce (page 32), is another way to add richness.

When it comes to meat, use tender cuts that lend themselves to dry-heat cooking methods like broiling, pan-broiling, sautéing, and stir-frying. True, tender cuts of meat are more expensive than tough ones, but you can cook them with lots of vegetables, as in Beef and Vegetable Stir-Fry (page 85) or keep meat portion sizes small to economize. Consider serving one or two meatless meals a week, either a rice salad or a pilaf, an egg dish, or pasta, and splurging at other times.

A secret to having quick weeknight meals is having a well-stocked larder. It's an old-fashioned word but a very contemporary concept. Keep an assortment of dried herbs and spices, plenty of oil (preferably extra-virgin olive oil because unlike other cooking oils it adds a flavor of its own), canned tomatoes, rice, and pasta in the cupboard, garlic in the vegetable bin, and parsley and lemon—two of the more piquant all-purpose seasonings there are—in the produce drawer of the refrigerator. Keep canned stock handy.

Labor-saving devices like the food processor and electric beaters save time too. They make it possible to whip up Peanut Butter Cupcakes with Chocolate Satin Frosting (page 105) or Tapioca Custard with Cocoa Whipped Cream (page 107) in a jiffy.

Asian Ingredients

- Chili oil
- Fermented black beans
- Fish sauce
- Hoisin sauce
- Oyster sauce
- Rice vinegar
- Rice wine
- Soy sauce
- Szechuan peppercorns
- Toasted sesame oil

Using Quick Weeknight Meals

All the recipes in this book were created with the home cook in mind. They are modern in spirit but not trendy, and they work the first time and every time. Master traditional favorites like Sloppy Joe (page 103) and Stovetop Macaroni and Cheese (page 37) and you'll have added two crowd pleasers to your everyday repertoire. Try a vegetarian specialty such as Brown Rice and Tofu Salad with Orange Sesame Dressing (page 23) for a change of pace.

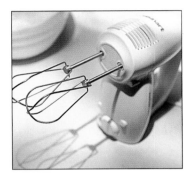

Each of the main recipes pictured can be the centerpiece of a weeknight meal. Some dishes, like Sautéed Veal Medallions on Arugula Tomato Salad (page 93), are a meal in one. Serve an ear of corn with the Crabcakes (page 57) or Green Beans with Sautéed Mushrooms (page 37) with the macaroni and cheese. Or mix and match, substituting Roasted Asparagus (page 97) or Parslied Carrots (page 43) for the green beans. Salade Niçoise (page 11) and the other main-course salads only need bread to round out the meal. Sometimes a green salad will suffice, as with Pan-Seared Steak with Smoky Onions (page 83).

Each main dish or dessert comes with a Shopping List, which tells you at a glance if you have everything you need and what you may have to buy. Step-by-Step photos make it easy to tackle unfamiliar cooking tasks and ingredients. Kitchen Tips and Helpful Hints highlight useful information about the recipes and ingredients.

To make the most of the recipes that follow, take stock of your refrigerator and rummage through your kitchen cabinets, then select a recipe according to the ingredients you've found. Or, in a few minutes of your spare time, browse through Quick Weeknight Meals and plan to shop for a busy week's worth of suppers ahead of time. We hope you'll take both approaches. Cooking is a creative endeavor and one of life's simplest and most rewarding activities, especially when it brings pleasure to you and yours.

Salade Niçoise

Salade Niçoise

You can depart from tradition and substitute grilled fresh tuna, salmon, or swordfish for the canned tuna.

4 to 6 servings

Cook in a large pot of boiling salted water until tender, about 20 minutes:
6 small red new potatoes

Remove with a slotted spoon, let cool, cut into ½-inch-thick slices, and place in a medium bowl. Meanwhile, add to the pot and boil until bright green but still crisp, 2 to 3 minutes:
1 pound green beans, trimmed

Drain, refresh under cold running water, drain again, and add to the potatoes. Whisk together in a small bowl:
3 tablespoons red wine vinegar
2 teaspoons Dijon mustard
Salt and ground black pepper to taste

Add in a slow, steady stream, whisking constantly:
6 tablespoons olive oil, preferably extra virgin

Drizzle about one-quarter of the dressing over the potatoes and beans and gently toss to coat, being careful not to break the potato slices. Arrange on a large platter:
1 head Boston lettuce, separated into leaves, washed, and dried

Arrange on top of the lettuce:
2 large ripe tomatoes, cut into 8 wedges each

Drizzle another quarter of the dressing on top. Arrange the green beans and potatoes on the platter along with:
5 hard-boiled eggs, halved lengthwise

Place in the center of the salad:
One 6-ounce can tuna, preferably oil packed, drained and flaked

Drizzle the remaining dressing over all. Scatter over the top:
½ cup Niçoise olives
¼ cup minced fresh parsley
2 tablespoons drained capers
2 to 4 anchovy fillets, rinsed and patted dry (optional)
Salt and ground black pepper to taste

Serve immediately.

White Bean Salad with Green Olives

Add a can of tuna to this salad and you can set the table for lunch or supper.

4 to 6 servings

Combine in a medium bowl:
3 cups cooked white kidney beans (about 1 cup dried) or other white beans, rinsed and drained if canned
2 small celery stalks, thinly sliced
15 Spanish olives, pitted and sliced
2 tablespoons chopped fresh tarragon or parsley

Whisk together:
1 tablespoon red wine vinegar
1 clove garlic, minced
½ teaspoon sweet paprika
¼ teaspoon salt

Whisk in:
3 to 4 tablespoons olive oil, preferably extra virgin

Pour the dressing over the bean mixture and toss gently to coat. Season with:
Ground black pepper to taste

Serve at room temperature.

Cobb Salad

Cobb Salad

This close cousin to chef's salad was created in the mid-1920s by restaurateur Bob Cobb at his Brown Derby Restaurant in Los Angeles.

4 to 6 servings

Mash together in a small bowl until a paste is formed:
1 clove garlic, peeled
¼ teaspoon salt

Whisk in:
⅓ cup red wine vinegar
1 tablespoon fresh lemon juice
¼ cup Roquefort or other blue cheese, crumbled
Salt and ground black pepper to taste

Add in a slow, steady stream, whisking constantly:
⅔ cup olive oil

Line a platter with:
1 head Bibb lettuce, separated into leaves, washed, and dried

Arrange on top of the lettuce leaves:
1 large bunch watercress (tough stems trimmed off), washed, dried, and coarsely chopped
1 ripe avocado, peeled and diced
4 to 6 cups diced cooked chicken or turkey breast
6 to 8 slices bacon, cooked until crisp and crumbled
3 hard-boiled eggs, diced
3 medium tomatoes, coarsely chopped
¼ cup finely snipped fresh chives
¼ cup Roquefort or other blue cheese, crumbled

Lightly drizzle the vinaigrette over the salad.

Serve, passing the remaining vinaigrette separately.

Reduced-Fat Cobb Salad

6 servings

Whisk together until smooth:
½ cup low-fat mayonnaise
½ cup buttermilk
2 shallots, minced
2 tablespoons minced fresh parsley
1 teaspoon minced fresh tarragon
Salt and ground black pepper to taste

Toss with half of the dressing:
1 small head Bibb lettuce, washed, dried, and shredded
1 cup fresh parsley leaves
1 small bunch watercress (tough stems trimmed off), washed, dried, and coarsely chopped

Place the greens on a platter and arrange in rows on top:
1 whole chicken breast, poached, skinned, boned, and shredded
4 plum tomatoes, peeled, seeded, and diced
½ ripe avocado, peeled and diced
¼ cup finely snipped fresh chives

Drizzle the remaining dressing over the salad and sprinkle with:
4 slices turkey bacon, cooked until crisp and crumbled
2 tablespoons finely crumbled Roquefort or other blue cheese

Serve immediately.

STEP-BY-STEP
Seeding an Avocado

Using a sharp knife, cut the avocado lengthwise around the seed. Grasp each half and twist to open. Separate the two halves, exposing the seed.

Sink a heavy knife into the seed. Holding the avocado half in the palm of your hand, lift out the seed.

Chinese Chicken Salad

Chinese Chicken Salad

Be sure to reserve some of the juice from the mandarin oranges, as it adds a delicious sweet tang to the dressing.

4 servings

Combine in a large bowl:
- **4 cups thin strips cooked chicken (about 1 pound cooked)**
- **1 cup canned mandarin oranges, drained, juice reserved**
- **⅔ cup sliced scallions**
- **½ cup chopped roasted unsalted peanuts**

Whisk together in a small bowl until well blended:
- **⅔ cup reserved mandarin orange juice**
- **½ cup peanut oil**
- **2 tablespoons fresh lemon juice**
- **1½ teaspoons chili oil (optional)**
- **1 teaspoon minced peeled fresh ginger**
- **½ teaspoon salt, or to taste**
- **¼ teaspoon ground Szechuan peppercorns**

Pour ½ cup dressing over the chicken mixture and toss to combine. Taste and adjust the seasonings. Serve the salad over:
- **4 cups shredded Chinese (Napa) cabbage**

Top with:
- **½ cup chopped roasted unsalted peanuts**
- **1 cup chow mein noodles**

Drizzle the remaining dressing over the salad and serve.

Chicken or Turkey Salad

For the ultimate chicken or turkey salad, roast the poultry on the bone, let it cool enough to handle, and shred or chop the meat into bite-sized pieces or large chunks. Be sure to include plenty of both dark and light meat for best flavor.

4 to 6 servings

Combine in a medium bowl:
- **2 cups diced cooked chicken or turkey**
- **1 cup diced celery**

Combine with:
- **½ to 1 cup mayonnaise**
- **Salt and ground black pepper to taste**

Serve on a bed of:
- **Lettuce leaves**

If desired, garnish with:
- **1 tablespoon chopped fresh parsley or tarragon**

Curried Chicken or Turkey Salad

Prepare Chicken or Turkey Salad, left, replacing the celery with ¼ cup each raisins and chopped toasted walnuts or almonds and 2 chopped scallions. Use Curry Mayonnaise, 121.

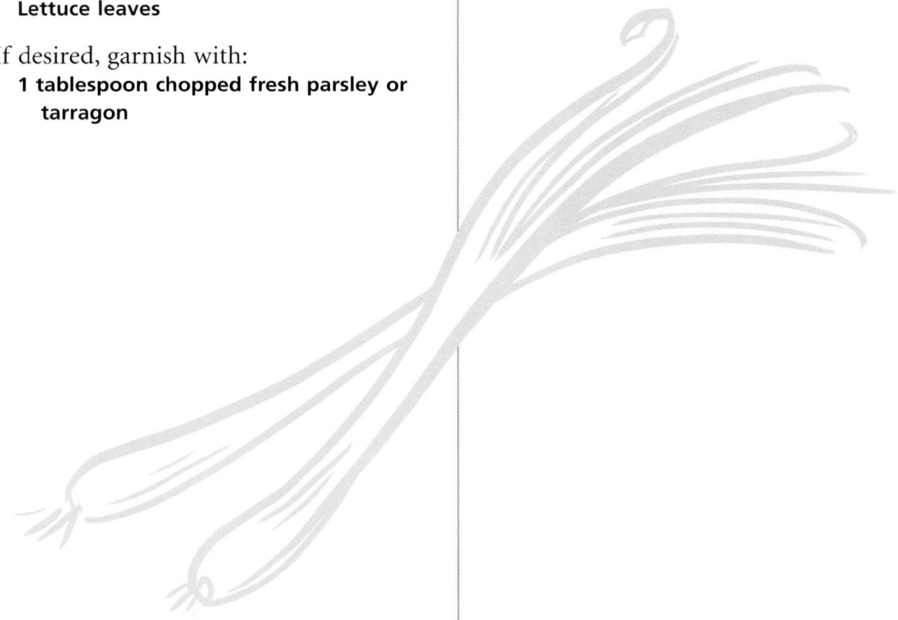

Pasta Salad with Grilled Chicken and Avocado

Pasta Salad with Grilled Chicken and Avocado

A thoroughly American treatment for pasta using favorite foods—grilled chicken and avocado. The dish can also be made with leftover baked or broiled chicken.

4 to 6 servings

Combine well in a large serving bowl:
- **3 boneless, skinless chicken breast halves (about 1 pound), grilled and cut into thin strips**
- **1 pound fusilli, cooked until tender but firm, rinsed with cool water, and drained**
- **1 large ripe avocado, peeled and finely diced**
- **3 medium, ripe tomatoes, seeded and chopped**
- **4 scallions, thinly sliced**
- **2 cloves garlic, finely minced**
- **¼ cup drained capers**
- **¼ cup chopped fresh basil, cilantro, or parsley**
- **¼ cup olive oil, or more to taste**
- **Juice of 1 lemon**
- **Salt and ground black pepper to taste**

Serve at room temperature.

HELPFUL HINT
Keeping Avocado Fresh

It is best to serve the Pasta Salad with Grilled Chicken and Avocado soon after it is made because the avocado tends to darken. If you need to make it ahead, dice and add the avocado just before serving.

Tortellini (or Ravioli) Salad

4 to 6 servings

Toss together gently in a large bowl:
- **1 pound tortellini or small cheese ravioli, cooked until tender but firm, rinsed with cool water, and drained**
- **2 pounds ripe tomatoes, peeled, seeded, and very coarsely chopped**
- **One 16-ounce jar marinated artichoke hearts, drained and quartered**
- **½ cup Niçoise or other oil-cured black olives, pitted and coarsely chopped**
- **3 tablespoons drained capers (optional)**
- **½ cup small fresh basil leaves, torn into pieces**

Season with:
- **2 to 3 drops red wine vinegar**
- **Salt and ground black pepper to taste**

Let cool for several minutes, then add:
- **4 ounces mozzarella cheese (preferably fresh), cut into ½-inch cubes**

Toss again.

Serve warm or at room temperature.

STEP-BY-STEP
Peeling, Seeding, and Juicing a Tomato

Plunge a tomato with a small X cut into the bottom skin into boiling water for 15 to 30 seconds. Lift out and transfer to a bowl of ice water.

Pull back the skin with a small knife, starting at the X and continuing around to the stem end. The skin will slip off easily. If not, put the tomato back into boiling water for 10 seconds.

Cut the tomato in half crosswise. Holding a half over a strainer set in a pot or bowl, gently squeeze to remove the seeds and juice.

Thai Beef Salad

Thai Beef Salad

Refreshing, aromatic salads are typical of Thai cooking.

6 servings

Bring to a boil in a large pot:
12 cups water

Add:
1½ pounds beef tenderloin, trimmed of fat and tied

Cover and cook at a steady simmer for 15 to 18 minutes for medium-rare. Remove the beef, cover with a damp dishtowel, and let cool to room temperature. Meanwhile, combine in a salad bowl:
3 bunches watercress (tough stems trimmed off), washed and dried
1¼ cups fresh mint leaves
1¼ cups fresh cilantro leaves
2 bunches radishes, thinly sliced
1 medium red onion, thinly sliced
2 tablespoons thin strips lemon zest

Cover and refrigerate until ready to serve. Whisk together in a small bowl:
½ cup vegetable oil
½ cup fresh lime juice
3 tablespoons fish sauce (optional)
1 tablespoon soy sauce
1½ teaspoons sugar
Red pepper flakes to taste
Salt and ground black pepper to taste

Slice the beef crosswise ½ inch thick, then cut into ½-inch-thick strips. Add the beef and dressing to the watercress mixture, toss to coat and combine.

Serve immediately.

Thai Coconut Rice

Thai, or jasmine, rice is a long-grain rice with a soft, slightly sticky consistency. Often sold as street food throughout Asia, the rice is cooked in spiced coconut milk and wrapped in a banana leaf, making it a handy package—very much the Far Eastern version of fast food. If using domestically grown jasmine rice, there is no need to rinse it. Imported jasmine rice should probably be rinsed.

4 to 6 servings

Bring to a boil in a large saucepan:
1 cup canned unsweetened coconut milk and 1 cup water
1 cup jasmine rice
1 thin slice peeled fresh ginger
¾ teaspoon salt

Stir once, cover, and cook over very low heat until the liquid is absorbed and the rice is tender, about 20 minutes. Meanwhile lightly toast, stirring, in a small skillet over medium-low heat:
⅓ cup flaked or shredded unsweetened dried coconut

Sprinkle over the cooked rice along with:
Fresh cilantro leaves (optional)

Rice Salad with Chicken and Pistachios

Shopping List

Cooked chicken	Unsalted pistachios
Red onion	Rice
Fresh basil and flat-leaf parsley	Olive oil
Lemon	Capers

Rice Salad with Chicken and Pistachios

4 servings

Stir together in a medium bowl:
- 3 cups diced cooked chicken
- ¾ cup shelled unsalted pistachios
- 1 medium red onion, finely diced
- ½ cup chopped flat-leaf parsley
- 6 fresh basil leaves, chopped
- ¼ cup drained capers
- ⅓ cup olive oil
- Grated zest and juice of 1 lemon
- Salt and ground black pepper to taste

Add while still warm:
- 3 cups cooked long-grain white rice, 123 (about 1½ cups uncooked)

Toss well to combine.

Serve at room temperature.

Rice Salad with Chicken and Black Olives

This recipe can be used as a blueprint for many kinds of rice salads. Simmer the rice in chicken stock for more flavor. As a general rule, use 3 cups cooked rice for roughly an equal amount of other ingredients (vegetables, fruit, chicken, seafood, etc.), cooked, if necessary, and chopped into bite-sized pieces. Toss with about ½ cup dressing of your choice.

4 servings

Stir together in a medium bowl:
- 1½ cups diced cooked chicken
- ½ cup diced peaches (about 1 medium)
- ½ cup coarsely chopped pitted oil-cured black olives
- ½ cup diced red or yellow bell peppers

Add while still warm:
- 3 cups cooked long-grain white rice, 123 (about 1½ cups uncooked)
- ½ cup Fresh Herb Vinaigrette, 119

Toss well to combine.

Serve warm, at room temperature, or chilled.

Rice Salad with Sun-Dried Tomatoes

4 servings

Whisk together in a medium bowl:
- 6 oil-packed sun-dried tomato halves, minced
- 6 tablespoons olive oil
- 3 tablespoons balsamic vinegar
- 1 clove garlic, minced
- 1 teaspoon chili powder
- ¼ teaspoon ground cumin
- ¼ teaspoon ground coriander

Add while still warm:
- 3 cups cooked long-grain white rice, 123 (about 1½ cups uncooked)

Stir in:
- 4 oil-packed sun-dried tomato halves, diced
- ¼ cup pine nuts, toasted
- 4 scallions, minced
- Salt and ground black pepper to taste

Toss well to combine.

Serve warm or at room temperature.

Brown Rice and Tofu Salad

Shopping List

Extra-firm tofu
Brown basmati rice
Adzuki beans
Lettuce
Jalapeño pepper

Red and green bell
  peppers
Red onion
Garlic
Fresh ginger
Fresh cilantro

Orange juice
Canola oil
Toasted sesame oil
Seasoned rice
  vinegar
Sesame seeds

Brown Rice and Tofu Salad with Orange Sesame Dressing

Smoked tofu is also an excellent choice for this salad. Black beans or any other preferred beans can be substituted for the adzukis.

6 servings

Shake together in a tightly covered jar:

½ cup canola oil
4 teaspoons toasted sesame oil
⅓ cup orange juice
⅓ cup seasoned rice vinegar
1 small fresh jalapeño pepper, seeded and minced
1 teaspoon minced peeled fresh ginger
1 teaspoon minced garlic

Chill. Combine in a large bowl:

4 cups warm cooked brown basmati rice
One 10½-ounce package extra-firm tofu, pressed if desired, and cut into ¾-inch cubes
3 cups cooked adzuki beans (about 1 cup dried), rinsed and drained if canned
½ cup chopped red onions
1 cup chopped bell peppers, preferably half red and half green
¼ cup finely chopped fresh cilantro

Shake the dressing well, pour over the rice mixture, and toss well to coat. Season with:

Salt and ground black pepper to taste

Line a serving platter with:

Lettuce leaves

Spoon the salad on the leaves and sprinkle with:

1 tablespoon sesame seeds, toasted

KITCHEN TIP
Adzuki Beans

Also called aduki or azuki beans, these small, claret red, mild-tasting beans are used to make the red bean paste used in Chinese buns and other sweets. They add color contrast to grain salads and can be substituted for small red beans, although they are more fragile in texture and much lighter in taste. Their flavor is faintly reminiscent of black-eyed peas. Both adzukis and black-eyed peas are in the mung bean family. Simmer, covered, for 30 to 40 minutes.

HELPFUL HINT
Using Tofu

The tofu used for cooking, sometimes called "cotton" tofu, is labeled soft, firm, or extra firm, depending on how much liquid was drained off during processing. Firm and extra firm hold together better in the pot. Cooks commonly firm up tofu by pressing it under a weight for 30 to 60 minutes, depending on how much water the tofu starts out with and the desired firmness. The curd becomes denser and chewier, holds together better when sliced or cubed, and releases less flavor-diluting water. If you press soft (but not silken) tofu, you can substitute it for firm.

Cheese and Herb Souffléed Omelet

Savory Cheese and Herb Souffléed Omelet

This savory omelet is made without sugar.

4 servings

Preheat the oven to 375°F.

Combine and whisk until thick and light:
4 large egg yolks
Salt and ground black pepper to taste

In a separate bowl, beat until stiff but not dry:
4 large egg whites
Pinch of salt

Fold the yolk mixture gently into the whites. Melt in a 10-inch ovenproof skillet over medium heat:
1 to 2 tablespoons butter

When the foam has subsided, pour the egg mixture into the pan, spread evenly, and smooth the top. Shake the pan after a few seconds to discourage sticking and then cover the pan with a lid whose underside has been buttered to prevent sticking. Reduce the heat and cook for about 5 minutes. Remove the cover and sprinkle with:
2 tablespoons chopped herbs (chives, parsley, chervil, or a combination)
¼ cup grated cheese

Place the skillet in the oven until the top is set, 3 to 5 minutes. Either fold the omelet in half or slide it out onto a warmed plate. Serve the omelet with Tomato Sauce, 125, or Salsa Fresca, 125.

Souffléed Omelet (basic recipe)

4 servings

Preheat the oven to 375°F.

Combine and whisk until thick and light:
4 large egg yolks
3 tablespoons sugar

In a separate bowl, beat until stiff but not dry:
4 large egg whites
Pinch of salt

Fold the yolk mixture gently into the whites. Melt in a 10-inch ovenproof skillet over medium heat:
1 to 2 tablespoons butter

When the foam has subsided, pour the egg mixture into the pan, spread evenly, and smooth the top. Shake the pan after a few seconds to discourage sticking and then cover the pan with a lid whose underside has been buttered to prevent sticking. Reduce the heat and cook for about 5 minutes. Remove the cover and place the skillet in the oven until the top is set, 3 to 5 minutes. Either fold the omelet in half or slide it out onto a warmed plate and sprinkle with:
Powdered sugar

Serve immediately.

Making a Souffléed Omelet

Separate the eggs, dropping the yolks into a small bowl and the whites into a large bowl.

Whisk together the egg yolks and sugar. Beat the whites until stiff, but not dry, peaks form.

Pour the egg yolk mixture over the beaten whites. Fold in by cutting down into the whites with a spatula, scooping some up, and turning them over the yolks.

Melt the butter in the pan. When the foam subsides, pour in the eggs and spread them evenly to the sides.

Zucchini Frittata

Zucchini Frittata

A frittata is the Italian version of an omelet. It is more robust than the classic French omelet and a bit easier to handle. Frittatas are cooked in a heavy skillet over low heat until they are firm—not runny like a French omelet—and they are left open-faced, not folded. Instead of trying to flip the frittata, we recommend popping it into the oven or under the broiler to cook the top side. Served in wedges, frittatas are delicious hot, warm, or at room temperature.

4 servings

Heat in a large skillet over medium heat:
   2 tablespoons olive oil

Add and cook, stirring, until golden brown:
   1 cup thinly sliced onions

Add and cook until lightly browned, about 10 minutes:
   3 medium zucchini, thinly sliced

Season with:
   ¼ teaspoon salt
   ⅛ teaspoon ground black pepper

Transfer the vegetables to a strainer to drain off the excess oil. Let cool completely.

Preheat the broiler.

Meanwhile, beat together until smooth:
   5 eggs
   ½ teaspoon salt
   Pinch of ground black pepper

Add the cooled zucchini and onion mixture along with:
   ½ cup grated Parmesan cheese (optional)
   1 tablespoon finely shredded fresh basil
   1 tablespoon minced fresh parsley

Heat in a large, ovenproof skillet over medium heat:
   2 tablespoons olive oil or butter

When hot, pour in the egg mixture. Reduce the heat and cook until the bottom is set, then place under the broiler for 30 to 60 seconds to finish cooking. A traditional frittata is not browned. Loosen the frittata with a spatula and slide it onto a plate.

Chard Sautéed with Garlic

4 to 6 servings

Remove the stems from:
   2 medium bunches red or green chard (about 1½ pounds)

Cut the stems into ½-inch pieces. Coarsely chop the leaves; rinse well, but do not dry. Heat in a large skillet over medium-low heat until the oil smells good and the garlic is just beginning to color:
   2 tablespoons extra-virgin olive oil
   2 cloves garlic, thinly sliced
   1 small dried red chili pepper, crumbled, or ¼ to ½ teaspoon red pepper flakes (optional)

Add the chard stems and season with:
   Salt to taste

Cook, stirring occasionally, until the stems are nearly tender, about 2 minutes. Add the chard leaves and cook, partially covered, until both the leaves and the stems are tender, 3 to 5 minutes more. Season with:
   Juice of ½ lemon or 1½ tablespoons red wine vinegar

Taste again for salt. Serve in a bowl, surrounded with:
   Lemon wedges

Or instead of salt and lemon, dot with:
   Soy Sauce Butter, 122

Crustless Ham and Cheese Quiche, left, Crustless Quiche Lorraine, right

Crustless Quiche Lorraine

Any quiche can be made crustless with the following recipe. If you use cheese, toss it with a tablespoon of all-purpose flour first to coat. Traditional quiche Lorraine contains no cheese.

One 10-inch quiche; 6 servings

Position a rack in the center or upper third of the oven. Preheat the oven to 400°F. Butter a 10-inch glass pie pan or ceramic quiche pan.

Cook in a heavy skillet over medium heat, stirring constantly, until the fat is almost rendered but the bacon is not yet crisp:

4 ounces sliced bacon, cut into 1-inch pieces

Drain on paper towels.

Beat together until well combined:
4 large eggs
1½ cups light cream
1 tablespoon chopped fresh herbs, or 1 teaspoon dried (optional)
½ teaspoon salt
¼ teaspoon freshly grated or ground nutmeg
Ground black pepper to taste

Add the bacon and stir well to distribute evenly in the custard. Pour the mixture into the prepared pan and bake until set, golden, and a knife inserted in the center comes out clean, about 30 minutes. Let rest for 10 minutes to settle, then cut into wedges and serve.

Crustless Ham and Cheese Quiche

Prepare Crustless Quiche Lorraine, opposite, substituting 1 cup chopped ham and 1 cup grated Gruyère or other cheese for the cooked bacon.

Crustless Broccoli Quiche

Sauté ½ red onion, chopped, and 1 clove garlic, minced, in olive oil until soft. Blanch and drain ⅔ cup broccoli florets. Prepare Crustless Quiche Lorraine, opposite, substituting the onions, broccoli, and ¾ cup grated Gruyère or other cheese for the cooked bacon.

Reduced-Fat Quiche

Prepare Crustless Quiche Lorraine, opposite, omitting the cooked bacon. Substitute 3 egg whites for 2 of the whole eggs and 1¼ cups milk plus ¼ cup light cream for the cream. Bake the quiche at 325°F in a water bath until set in the center and a knife inserted in the center comes out clean, 40 to 55 minutes. If desired, place the quiche briefly under the broiler to brown the top before serving.

HELPFUL HINT
The Water Bath

The water bath, also known as the bain-marie or "Maria's bath," is the cook's principal means of managing heat during the cooking of custards. By baking a quiche in a larger pan of water, the cook partially insulates the quiche from the oven's heat and thereby protects it from overcooking. To bake quiche in a water bath, all you need is a roasting pan large enough to accommodate the quiche comfortably. The quiche pan should not touch the hot roasting pan walls. Either set a cake rack in the pan or cover the pan bottom with a dish towel or several layers of paper towels; the rack or towel(s) will prevent the quiche from coming into direct contact with the hot pan bottom. Arrange the quiche in the dry pan, slip the pan into a preheated 325°F oven, and immediately pour enough scalding-hot tap water into the pan to come one-half to two-thirds of the way up the sides of the quiche pan. (Some cooks prefer to pour the water into the pan before setting the pan in the oven. This is fine so long as you are able to hold the pan steady and level and thereby avoid splashing water into the quiche.)

Tagliatelle with Wilted Greens

Tagliatelle with Wilted Greens

Make this dish as spicy as you like by using more or fewer chili peppers. Remember, much of a chili's heat is in the seeds, so that removing them will temper the dish.

4 to 8 servings

Bring to a rolling boil in a large pot:
**6 quarts water
1 tablespoon salt**

Add and cook until tender but firm:
**1¼ pounds fresh tagliatelle,
or 1 pound dried**

Meanwhile, heat in a large skillet or wok over medium heat:
2 to 4 tablespoons olive oil

Add and cook until barely browned:
**¼ cup minced onion
4 cloves garlic, chopped
1 to 3 fresh hot chili peppers, seeded and finely diced**

Increase the heat to high and drop in:
4 cups loosely packed fresh arugula or mixed tart salad greens

Cook, stirring, until the greens are wilted. Drain the pasta and toss it with the greens, adding:
**Salt and ground black pepper to taste
Shavings of Pecorino Romano cheese or crumbled fresh goat cheese**

Serve immediately.

Straw and Hay (Paglia e Fieno)

This quick, but luxuriously good, dish gets its name from the mix of green and yellow fettuccine.

4 to 8 servings

Bring to a rolling boil in a large pot:
**6 quarts water
1 tablespoon salt**

Add and cook until tender but firm:
**12 ounces fresh spinach fettuccine, or 8 ounces dried
12 ounces fresh egg fettuccine, or 8 ounces dried**

Meanwhile, heat in a large skillet over medium heat:
1 tablespoon butter

Add and cook for 1 minute:
2 ounces prosciutto, chopped

Add and boil for 2 minutes:
1 cup heavy cream

Stir in and cook 2 minutes more:
1 package (10 ounces) frozen peas

Drain the pasta and add it to the skillet along with:
**2 ounces prosciutto, chopped
1 cup freshly grated Parmesan cheese
Salt and ground black pepper to taste**

Serve immediately.

STEP-BY-STEP
Seeding a Hot Chili Pepper

Wearing rubber gloves, remove the stem of the hot chili pepper and cut the pepper in half lengthwise. Scrape away the seeds and cut away the inner membrane.

Tomato and Mozzarella Salad (Insalata Caprese)

Named for the island of Capri, where it was perhaps first made, this gloriously simple salad is popular all over Italy and is increasingly so in the United States.

4 to 6 servings

Arrange, alternating slices, on a platter:
**4 large ripe tomatoes, cut into ½-inch-thick slices
12 ounces mozzarella cheese, cut into ¼-inch-thick slices**

Sprinkle with:
1½ cups fresh basil leaves, chopped

Drizzle over the salad:
**½ cup olive oil, preferably extra virgin
Salt to taste**

Serve at once or let stand at room temperature for up to 1 hour before serving. In either case, do not refrigerate the salad.

Clockwise from upper right, Pesto Sauce, Porcini and Red Wine Sauce, Maria's Twenty-Minute Tomato Sauce

Pesto Sauce

This classic sauce from Genoa needs to be made with fresh basil. Pesto is traditionally tossed with trenette, a flat ribbon pasta similar to linguine but fresh. Sometimes green beans and sliced potatoes are cooked along with the pasta in the same water, making the dish more robust. If freezing, add the nuts and cheese after thawing.

Enough for 1 pound pasta

Process to a rough paste in a food processor:

    2 cups loosely packed fresh basil leaves
    ⅓ cup pine nuts
    2 medium cloves garlic, peeled
    ½ cup grated Parmesan cheese

With the machine running, slowly pour through the feed tube:

    ½ cup extra-virgin olive oil

If the sauce seems dry (it should be a thick paste), add a little more olive oil. Season with:

    Salt and ground black pepper to taste

Use immediately or store in a covered glass jar in the refrigerator for up to 1 week.

Maria's Twenty-Minute Tomato Sauce

Enough for 1 pound pasta

Heat in a medium saucepan over medium heat:

    2 tablespoons extra-virgin olive oil

Add:

    1 medium onion, minced
    2 medium carrots, peeled and minced
    2 cloves garlic, minced

Cook, stirring, until softened, about 5 minutes. Stir in:

    One 28-ounce can whole tomatoes, with juice, broken into pieces
    1 tablespoon dried basil
    1 to 2 teaspoons dried oregano

Simmer, uncovered, until the sauce is thickened, about 10 minutes. Remove to a food processor and pulse until smooth. Return to the saucepan and stir in:

    1 to 2 teaspoons sugar
    ½ to 1 teaspoon red pepper flakes
    Salt and ground black pepper to taste

Heat through, about 5 minutes.

Porcini and Red Wine Sauce

A robust and meaty-tasting sauce with little or no meat and the haunting woodsy taste of porcini mushrooms.

Enough for 1 pound pasta

Soak in hot water to cover until softened, about 20 minutes:

1½ ounces dried porcini mushrooms, thoroughly rinsed

Remove the mushrooms with a slotted spoon and chop. Strain the soaking liquid through a sieve lined with a paper towel. Heat in a large skillet over medium-high heat:

2 tablespoons extra-virgin olive oil
2 ounces pancetta, finely chopped (optional)

Add:

½ medium onion, minced
Zest of ½ lemon, cut into very thin strips
4 fresh or dried sage leaves

Cook, stirring, until the onions are softened. Add the porcini along with:

8 ounces button mushrooms, wiped clean and thinly sliced

Increase the heat to high and cook, stirring, until the mushrooms are golden brown. Stir in:

1 clove garlic, minced

Stir in the porcini soaking liquid. Simmer briskly until the liquid is reduced to a glaze. Stir in and reduce again to a glaze:

1 cup dry red wine

Stir in:

1 cup chicken stock

Season with:

Salt and ground black pepper to taste

STEP-BY-STEP
Preparing Dried Mushrooms

Rinse the dried mushrooms, place in a bowl, and pour on hot water to cover. Let stand for 20 minutes.

Remove the mushrooms from the liquid with a slotted spoon and transfer to paper towels to drain. Leave the liquid in the bowl.

Using a heavy chef's knife, chop the mushrooms, discarding hard stems.

Line a sieve with a damp paper towel and place over a bowl. Strain the liquid through the sieve.

HELPFUL HINT
Rules for Cooking Pasta

Pasta should be cooked and eaten; never prepare it ahead. Cook and immediately toss with sauce.

Count on 6 quarts boiling water seasoned with about 1 tablespoon salt per pound of pasta. Eliminate salt only if absolutely necessary. Delicate filled pastas or large pieces need 9 to 12 quarts water. Do not use oil—it achieves nothing.

Unless it is outrageously long, do not break pasta before cooking.

Cook pasta at a fierce boil, stirring often. Fresh pasta cooks in several seconds to several minutes, while dried pasta takes longer. Taste for doneness. There should be no raw flour taste and some firmness to the bite (Italians call this al dente). Soft, mushy pasta is thrown out, never eaten.

Immediately drain cooked pasta into a large colander and toss to rid it of all water. Then quickly combine with sauce.

Never rinse pasta unless it will be baked or served cool in a salad. Starches clinging to the surface of the noodles help them meld with the sauces.

Pasta is best hot, so warm up its serving bowl and dishes if at all possible.

Pasta salads are best cool or at room temperature, not cold.

Johnny Marzetti Spaghetti Pie

Johnny Marzetti Spaghetti Pie

There are many variations to be found throughout the Midwest of this Sunday night pasta casserole made famous at Marzetti's restaurant in Columbus, Ohio. All contain chopped beef, tomatoes, and pasta, but some add mushrooms, olives and/or mozzarella. Think of it as a Sloppy Joe with an Italian accent. Any type of dried pasta can be used in this dish.

6 to 8 servings

In a 5- to 6-quart Dutch oven, brown over medium heat until the beef loses most of its pink color, about 8 minutes:
   1½ pounds ground beef chuck
   1 large onion, chopped
   1 green bell pepper, chopped
   2 cloves garlic, minced

Add:
   One 35-ounce can Italian tomatoes, with juice, chopped
   One 12-ounce can tomato sauce
   1 teaspoon dried oregano
   1 bay leaf
   Salt and ground black pepper to taste

Bring to a boil, reduce the heat to medium-low, and simmer, stirring frequently, about 20 minutes.

Preheat the oven to 350°F. Bring to a rolling boil in a large pot:
   6 quarts water
   1 tablespoon salt

Add and cook until tender but firm:
   1 pound spaghetti, ziti, or other dried pasta

Drain well and add to the sauce along with:
   1 cup shredded sharp Cheddar cheese

Mix well and top with:
   1 cup fresh breadcrumbs, lightly toasted
   1 cup shredded sharp Cheddar cheese

Bake until the top is lightly browned and the casserole is bubbling, about 30 minutes. Let stand for 5 minutes before serving.

Wilted Spinach or Chard

Combined with ricotta cheese, this makes an excellent filling for ravioli.

2 or 3 servings

Wash thoroughly but do not dry:
   12 well-packed cups spinach or chard leaves or a combination

Coarsely chop, then place in a large skillet. Season with:
   Salt to taste

Cook, stirring frequently, over medium heat until completely wilted but still bright green, about 5 minutes. Remove to a serving dish and toss with:
   Extra-virgin olive oil
   Dash of white wine vinegar, red wine vinegar, or lemon juice
   Ground black pepper to taste

Serve immediately.

Stovetop Macaroni and Cheese

Shopping List

Elbow macaroni

Extra-sharp Cheddar cheese

Eggs

Butter, preferably unsalted

Evaporated milk

Dry mustard

Ground red pepper

Stovetop Macaroni and Cheese

Very creamy and very cheesy. The size of the pot is essential in this recipe—it must be big for the sauce to thicken correctly. If you do not have a 7-quart pot, you can cook the elbow macaroni in any pot, then prepare the cheese sauce and finish the dish in a 12-inch skillet.

4 to 6 servings

Bring to a rolling boil in a large pot:
   12 cups water
   1 tablespoon salt

Add and cook just until tender:
   2 cups elbow macaroni (8 ounces)

Drain and return to the pot. Add:
   4 tablespoons (½ stick) unsalted butter, cut into small pieces

Stir until well blended. Add and stir together until smooth:
   One 12-ounce can evaporated milk
   12 ounces extra-sharp Cheddar cheese, shredded
   2 large eggs, lightly beaten
   1 teaspoon dry mustard dissolved in 1 teaspoon water
   ¾ teaspoon salt
   ½ teaspoon ground red pepper, or to taste

Set the pot over very low heat and, stirring constantly, bring the mixture to the first bubble of a simmer, 5 to 10 minutes. It should thicken noticeably. This may take several minutes. Increase the heat slightly if the sauce is still soupy after 5 minutes, but watch it very carefully. Do not overheat (above 170°F), or the sauce will curdle. Serve immediately. If you are not ready to serve, remove the pot from the heat, cover the surface with plastic wrap, cover the pot, and let stand at room temperature.

Green Beans with Sautéed Mushrooms

3 or 4 servings

Steam until tender, 10 to 15 minutes:
   1 pound green beans, trimmed, halved if desired

Meanwhile, heat in a large nonstick skillet:
   1 tablespoon extra-virgin olive oil

Add:
   8 ounces mushrooms, wiped clean and sliced
   1 tablespoon minced shallots or onions

Cook over medium heat until the mushrooms are tender, 3 to 5 minutes. Add the steamed beans to the skillet along with:
   Salt and ground black pepper to taste

Toss the mixture well to heat the beans through, then serve.

STEP-BY-STEP
Steaming Green Beans

Layer trimmed green beans in a steamer basket set over 1 to 2 inches of boiling water. Cover and cook until tender but still crisp.

Halfway through the steaming time (after 5 to 7 minutes), turn the beans so that the ones on the bottom cook as evenly as the ones on top.

Clockwise from right, Egg Noodles with Sour Cream and Chives, Egg Noodles with Garlic and Breadcrumbs, Egg Noodles with Brown Butter and Nuts

Buttered Egg Noodles

This very quick and easy noodle recipe will keep the kids at the supper table.

6 to 8 servings

Bring to a rolling boil in a large saucepan:
- **12 cups water**
- **1 tablespoon salt**

Add and cook until tender but firm:
- **1 pound egg noodles**

Fresh noodles will take as long as 5 minutes, depending upon how thick they are. If using dried noodles, follow the package directions. Drain the noodles and return to the pot. Add:
- **8 tablespoons (1 stick) unsalted butter, melted**
- **Salt and ground black pepper to taste**

Toss to coat and serve in warmed bowls.

Egg Noodles with Pot Cheese

6 to 8 servings

Toss together in the noodle cooking pot:
- **1 pound egg noodles, cooked until tender but firm**
- **8 tablespoons (1 stick) unsalted butter, melted**
- **1 pound pot or cottage cheese**
- **Salt and ground black pepper to taste**

Heat through over low heat.
Serve garnished with:
- **Crumbled bacon (optional)**
- **Chopped fresh parsley or snipped fresh dill**

Egg Noodles with Sour Cream and Chives

6 to 8 servings

Combine in a medium saucepan:
- **8 tablespoons (1 stick) unsalted butter, melted**
- **8 ounces sour cream or plain yogurt**
- **¼ cup minced onions**
- **2 tablespoons finely snipped fresh chives**
- **2 tablespoons chopped fresh parsley**
- **1 clove garlic, minced**

Cook gently for about 5 minutes.
Toss with:
- **1 pound egg noodles, cooked until tender but firm**

Serve immediately.

Egg Noodles with Garlic and Breadcrumbs

6 to 8 servings

Melt in a medium skillet until the foam subsides:
- **4 to 8 tablespoons (½ to 1 stick) unsalted butter**

Add:
- **1 cup dry unseasoned breadcrumbs**
- **1 to 2 cloves garlic, minced**

Cook, stirring, until the breadcrumbs begin to brown. Stir in:
- **1 tablespoon chopped fresh parsley**

Toss with:
- **1 pound egg noodles, cooked until tender but firm**

Serve immediately.

Egg Noodles with Brown Butter and Nuts

6 to 8 servings

Place in a small pan:
- **8 tablespoons (1 stick) unsalted butter**

Gradually brown the butter over medium heat until golden brown and a nutty aroma arises. Add, if desired, any one or all of the following:
- **¼ cup chopped nuts, such as cashews, roasted peanuts, pecans, toasted almonds, pine nuts, or toasted walnuts**
- **1 teaspoon minced garlic (optional)**
- **1 tablespoon chopped fresh herbs, or 1 teaspoon dried such as thyme, basil, chives, parsley, oregano, and/or tarragon (optional)**
- **Grated zest of small lemon (optional)**

Toss with:
- **1 pound egg noodles, cooked until tender but firm**

Serve immediately.

Soft Polenta with Mushroom Ragout

Shopping List

Yellow cornmeal

Assorted fresh
mushrooms

Onions

Garlic

Fresh or dried
rosemary

Fresh parsley

Butter, preferably
unsalted

Parmesan cheese

Olive oil

Balsamic vinegar

Tomato paste

Vegetable or
chicken stock,
if using

Black peppercorns

Soft Polenta with Butter and Cheese

This is the basic formula for stirred soft polenta. For more flavor, replace up to half of the water with chicken stock.

About 4 cups; 4 servings

Melt in a large saucepan over medium heat:
   3 tablespoons butter

Add and cook, stirring, until translucent, about 5 minutes:
   ½ cup finely chopped onions

Stir in and bring to a boil:
   3 cups water

Stir together:
   1 cup water
   1 cup yellow cornmeal

Gradually stir into the boiling water, reduce the heat to low, and cook, stirring constantly with a wooden spoon, until the polenta is very thick and leaves the side of the pan as it is stirred, about 25 minutes. Sprinkle with:
   2 tablespoons to ½ cup grated Parmesan cheese
   1 teaspoon salt, or to taste

Mushroom Ragout

Serve over soft polenta, rice, garlic-rubbed croutons, or popovers. For more intense flavor, soak ½ ounce dried mushrooms, chop, and add with the fresh mushrooms; use the soaking water for part of the liquid.

4 servings

Heat over medium-high heat in a large saucepan:
   1 tablespoon olive oil

Add and cook until golden, about 10 minutes:
   1 onion, diced

Remove and set aside. Heat in the same pan over medium heat:
   1 tablespoon olive oil

Add and cook until they begin to release their liquid:
   1 pound assorted fresh mushrooms, wiped clean and thickly sliced

Add the onions along with:
   2 cloves garlic, finely chopped
   1 teaspoon chopped fresh rosemary, or scant ½ teaspoon dried
   Salt and ground black pepper to taste

Cook until the mushrooms begin to brown, another 3 to 4 minutes. Stir in:
   1 tablespoon tomato paste

Increase the heat to high and cook, stirring, for 1 to 2 minutes more. Add:
   1½ cups vegetable stock, chicken stock, or water

Reduce the heat and simmer for 10 minutes. Stir in to form a sauce:
   2 tablespoons cold butter, cut into pieces
   1½ teaspoons balsamic vinegar

Garnish with:
   Grated Parmesan cheese (optional)
   Chopped fresh parsley

STEP-BY-STEP
Making Polenta

First, make a slurry: Stir together the cold water and cornmeal in a bowl until smooth. Using a slurry minimizes the risk of lumps.

Gradually stir the cornmeal slurry into the boiling water or stock over medium heat, then immediately reduce the heat to low.

Cook, stirring constantly with a wooden spoon, until the polenta is very thick and leaves the side of the pan as it is stirred.

Lentil and Rice Pilaf

Lentil and Rice Pilaf with Toasted Cumin Seeds

Lentils are the fastest-cooking dried legume and, for that reason, can be cooked with white rice into an interesting pilaf. Whole cumin seeds lend a wonderful aroma to the dish. Serve as a main course topped with cooked vegetables.

4 to 6 servings

Stir into a medium saucepan of boiling water:
- **½ cup lentils, picked over and rinsed**

Boil, uncovered, for 10 minutes; drain. Heat in a large saucepan or deep skillet over low heat:
- **2 tablespoons vegetable oil**

Add and cook just until sizzling, about 1 minute:
- **1 clove garlic, finely chopped**
- **½ teaspoon cumin seeds**

Add the lentils along with:
- **1 cup white basmati rice**

Stir to combine. Add:
- **2 cups chicken stock**
- **¼ to ½ teaspoon salt**

Bring to a boil. Stir once, cover, and cook over medium-low heat until the stock is absorbed and the rice and lentils are tender, about 15 minutes. Uncover and let stand for 5 minutes. Meanwhile, toast in a small skillet over medium heat:
- **¼ cup chopped walnuts**

Sprinkle over the pilaf and serve.

Parslied Carrots

A family favorite.

4 to 6 servings

Steam, or boil in salted water until tender, 7 to 10 minutes:
- **6 large carrots (about 1½ pounds), peeled and thinly sliced into rounds**

Drain and rinse to stop the cooking. Cook in a large skillet over medium heat until softened:
- **2 tablespoons finely diced shallots or onions**
- **2 tablespoons butter**

Add the cooked carrots along with:
- **½ teaspoon fresh lemon juice**
- **Salt to taste**
- **Paprika or ground black pepper to taste**

When the carrots are warmed through, toss them with:
- **2 tablespoons chopped fresh parsley**

Braised Celery Hearts

A luscious accompaniment.

4 servings

Arrange in a large skillet or Dutch oven:
- **1½ pounds celery hearts, washed, trimmed, and cut into 3- to 4-inch lengths**

Top with:
- **½ cup chicken or veal stock**
- **3 tablespoons fresh lemon juice**
- **2 tablespoons butter, cut into small pieces**
- **1 tablespoon sugar**
- **½ teaspoon salt**

KITCHEN TIP
Aromatic Rice

Numerous varieties of rice are called aromatic because they have a pronounced nutty fragrance due to a higher concentration of a natural compound found in all rice. The most famous of these is basmati, a long-grain rice, white or brown, grown in India, Pakistan, and now also the United States; it gives Indian pilafs their distinctive, and irresistible, fluffy texture and aroma. Jasmine is a long-grain white aromatic rice originally from Thailand and now grown in the United States as well; it cooks moist and tender but not fluffy, like a medium-grain rice, and has a lovely subtle perfume. Other popular American-grown aromatic rices are Texmati, white and brown, a type of basmati from Texas; Wehani, a long-grain brown variety from California; and Louisiana pecan, a white rice named for its aroma.

Bring the liquid to a boil, then cover closely with parchment paper or aluminum foil and then the lid. Simmer until tender, about 25 minutes. Transfer the celery to a platter and keep warm. Boil the remaining liquid over medium-high heat until reduced to about ½ cup. Add and cook for 1 minute:
- **1 tablespoon butter**

Pour this glaze over the celery and serve.

Fried Rice

Fried Rice

*F*ried rice is considered snack food by the Chinese and is never served as the main course at a Chinese meal. Americans like to eat fried rice as a main dish. It is popular as much for its taste as for its rapid preparation and versatility. Remember to always begin with cold cooked rice (a mixture of part white and part brown is excellent).

4 servings

Whisk together:
4 eggs
½ teaspoon salt

Heat a large nonstick skillet or wok over medium heat until hot enough to evaporate a drop of water on contact. Pour in and tilt the skillet to coat:
1 tablespoon vegetable oil

Heat until very hot. Add the eggs all at once and as they bubble up around the edges, push them to the center, tilting the skillet to cook the eggs evenly. Break the cooked eggs into clumps. When the eggs are set, remove to a bowl. Pour into the hot skillet and heat until hot:
2 tablespoons vegetable oil

Add and cook, stirring to coat the grains with oil, for 3 minutes:
3 to 4 cups cold cooked rice (1 to 1⅓ cups uncooked)
1 teaspoon minced peeled fresh ginger

Stir in the cooked eggs along with:
½ cup thin diagonal scallion slices

Serve immediately.

Stir-Fried Bok Choy with Mushrooms

4 to 6 servings

Place in a small bowl:
6 dried black or shiitake mushrooms

Pour over the mushrooms:
½ cup boiling water

Let soak for 20 minutes, stirring the mushrooms occasionally. While the mushrooms soak, prepare, keeping the stems separate from the leafy parts:
1½ to 2 pounds bok choy, bottoms trimmed, stalks washed, and cut into 2-inch pieces

In a small saucepan, warm over medium-low heat:
1 cup chicken stock
½ teaspoon salt
½ teaspoon sugar

Remove the mushrooms from their soaking liquid and reserve the liquid. Cut the mushrooms into ¼-inch-thick slices and set aside. In a small bowl, mix:
2 tablespoons reserved mushroom soaking liquid, strained
1 tablespoon Scotch whisky or Shaoxing wine
2 teaspoons cornstarch
¾ teaspoon ground white pepper

Heat in a wok or a large skillet over high heat:
3 tablespoons peanut oil

Add the reserved mushrooms and bok choy stems and cook, stirring often, for 3 to 5 minutes to soften. Add the reserved bok choy leaves and warmed chicken stock, cover, and steam until the leaves wilt, 1 to 2 minutes. Uncover and transfer the vegetables with a slotted spoon to a serving dish. Stir the reserved cornstarch mixture and whisk into the chicken stock. Bring to a boil, whisking, and add:
2 teaspoons toasted sesame oil

Stir well, pour the sauce over the vegetables, and serve.

Fish Steak Poached in White Wine

Fish Steaks Poached in White Wine

Use any fish steaks you like in this recipe: Salmon, cod, sturgeon, turbot, and halibut are all good. The poaching liquid can be reused. After you are finished cooking, boil it for 2 minutes, cool, strain, and refrigerate up to 3 days or freeze indefinitely. It pays to brighten it a bit with fresh herbs, spices, and vinegar each time you use it.

4 servings

Place in a deep skillet or casserole large enough to hold the fish in a single layer:

> **2 cups dry white wine**
> **2 cups water**
> **2 tablespoons rice, sherry, or white wine vinegar**
> **1 teaspoon salt**
> **10 black peppercorns**
> **10 coriander seeds**
> **2 whole cloves**
> **1 bay leaf**
> **1 clove garlic**
> **Several sprigs fresh parsley, thyme, or tarragon, or ½ teaspoon dried**

Bring to a boil, uncovered, over high heat; reduce the heat and simmer for 5 minutes. Place gently in the poaching liquid:

> **1½ to 2 pounds fish steaks (4 small or 2 large), rinsed and patted dry**

Cover the pan and adjust the heat so that the liquid is gently simmering; cook for 8 minutes, then check for doneness, right. Remove the fish when the flesh still clings a little bit to the bone and is slightly translucent. If desired, serve hot with parslied potatoes, or at room temperature, or chilled with:

> **A mayonnaise, 120 to 121, or a vinaigrette, 119**

Cucumber Salad

4 servings

Combine in a small bowl:

> **¼ cup rice vinegar**
> **4 teaspoons sesame seeds, toasted**
> **2 teaspoons sugar**

Add and toss to coat:

> **1 large cucumber, scrubbed or peeled if waxed, halved crosswise, and cut into thin strips or thinly sliced crosswise**

Cover and refrigerate until the salad is cold, about 1 hour. Serve.

HELPFUL HINT

How to Know When Fish Is Done

As a general guideline, cook fish for 8 to 9 minutes per inch of thickness.

The signs of doneness are a firming up of texture; the beginnings of flakiness; an opaque, whiter look throughout.

Remove the fish just before it reaches the stage at which you want to eat it; it will finish cooking between kitchen and plate.

All fish is cooked through at 137°F on an instant-read thermometer. Usually, 135°F leaves just a hint of translucence and more moisture and is done enough for most people. For tuna and other fish that you might prefer less well-done, try 120°F for starters.

Roasted Fish Fillet Spencer

Roasted Fish Fillets Spencer

This time-honored method of roasting fillets produces results similar to frying but with far less fuss and considerably less fat. Serve with lots of lemon or with Tartar Sauce, 121, or Salsa Verde Cruda, below.

4 servings

Position a rack in the upper third of the oven. Preheat the oven to 550°F. Lightly oil a baking sheet or shallow roasting pan.

Mix in a shallow bowl:
 **½ cup milk, warmed
 1 teaspoon salt**

Spread in a second shallow bowl:
 1 cup fresh breadcrumbs, toasted

Dip first in the milk mixture, then coat with the breadcrumbs:
 **1½ to 2 pounds cod or other thick
 white fillets, in 1 or 2 pieces, rinsed
 and patted dry**

Make sure the fillets are well coated, patting to help the crumbs adhere. Place the fillets on the baking sheet and drizzle over them:
 **2 tablespoons extra-virgin olive oil,
 melted butter, or melted bacon
 drippings**

Roast for 8 to 12 minutes, depending on the thickness of the fillets. Garnish with:
 **Minced fresh parsley
 Lemon wedges**

Salsa Verde Cruda

Intensely fresh, pungent, and herbal, this tomatillo salsa is the easiest salsa of all. It is especially good with fish, chicken, steamed or roasted vegetables, and eggs. However, since the onion is not rinsed and everything is whirled to a puree, it must be served within an hour of preparing for optimum quality. If left to sit, the raw onion will overpower the sauce.

About 2 cups

Combine in a food processor or blender and coarsely puree, leaving the mixture a little chunky:
 **8 ounces tomatillos, husked, rinsed, and
 coarsely chopped
 1 small white or red onion, coarsely
 chopped
 3 to 5 fresh green chili peppers (such
 as serrano or jalapeño), seeded and
 coarsely chopped**

STEP-BY-STEP
Preparing a Tomatillo

Peel off the papery husk of each tomatillo and discard. Rinse the tomatillo to remove the sticky covering that lies under the husk.

Carefully remove the tomatillo stem. Do not peel. The tomatillo is ready to be chopped.

 **1 clove garlic, peeled (optional)
 3 to 4 tablespoons fresh cilantro sprigs**

Remove to a medium bowl and stir in enough cold water to loosen the mixture to a saucelike consistency. Stir in:
 **1 teaspoon salt, or to taste
 ¾ teaspoon sugar (optional)**

Serve immediately.

Roasted Whole Red Snapper

Shopping List

Whole red snapper or
   other whole fish

Fresh parsley

Lemon

Extra-virgin olive oil

Sherry or other vinegar

Roasted Whole Red Snapper or Other Fish

Red snapper, grouper, blackfish, rockfish, or any other meaty fish is wonderful when roasted.

4 servings

Preheat the oven to 500°F. Cut 3 or 4 slashes in each side of:

1 red snapper or other whole fish (3 to 4 pounds), rinsed inside and out and patted dry

Combine and rub the fish inside and out with:

1 tablespoon extra-virgin olive oil
1 tablespoon sherry or other vinegar or fresh lemon juice

Season inside and out with:

Salt and ground black pepper to taste

Make sure to get some flavoring into the slashes. Line a shallow roasting pan with aluminum foil (to ease cleanup) and place the fish on a rack in the pan. Roast, undisturbed, until the meat is opaque right down to the bone, 25 to 35 minutes. (To check for doneness, see page 47.) Serve with:

Minced fresh parsley and lemon wedges, or a vinaigrette, 119

Carrot and Raisin Salad

If you have the time, crisp the peeled carrots on ice for an hour before grating.

4 servings

Combine in a medium bowl:

4 large carrots, peeled and coarsely grated
½ cup raisins
½ cup coarsely chopped pecans or unsalted roasted peanuts
2 teaspoons grated lemon zest
1 tablespoon fresh lemon juice
¾ teaspoon salt
Ground black pepper to taste

Pour over:

1 cup sour cream, or ½ cup sour cream and ½ cup mayonnaise

Toss well and serve.

Deep-Fried Fish Fillet and Hushpuppies

Deep-Fried Fillets, Southern Style

When you deep-fry whole fish, you must have a suitably large vessel and plenty of oil. This simple technique is fast and easy; just be sure to use firm-fleshed fish—catfish, red snapper, blackfish, dogfish, grouper, and the like, are best—and properly heated oil.

4 servings

Heat in a deep-fat fryer or deep, heavy pot over medium-high heat to 375°F:
> **2 inches corn, canola, olive, peanut, or other oil**

Mix in a shallow bowl:
> **1 cup cornmeal or all-purpose flour**
> **1 tablespoon chili powder (optional)**
> **Salt and ground black pepper to taste**

Coat with the seasoned cornmeal:
> **1½ to 2 pounds fish fillets, rinsed and thoroughly patted dry**

Pat the cornmeal onto the fish to help it adhere. Add the fish 1 piece at a time to the hot oil and increase the heat to high to maintain the temperature. Cook the fish in batches if the pot becomes crowded—it will not take long. Stir once or twice just to make sure the fillets are not sticking anywhere. Remove the fillets when they are golden brown. Drain on paper bags or paper towels. Serve immediately with:
> **Hushpuppies, right**
> **Tartar Sauce, 121**
> **Lemon wedges**

Hushpuppies

Fishermen used to fry this savory corn-meal batter in the same lard as the catfish. Legend has it that they threw some to their clamorous dogs with the admonition, "Hush, puppy!" These morsels consist of a crusty, golden brown exterior surrounding a tasty corn-and-onion-flavored center. They go particularly well with fried fish and barbecued dishes.

About 12 hushpuppies

Have ready a baking sheet lined with paper towels.

Whisk together thoroughly in a large bowl:
> **1⅔ cups cornmeal, preferably stone ground**
> **⅓ cup all-purpose flour**
> **2 teaspoons baking powder**
> **1 teaspoon sugar**
> **1 teaspoon ground black pepper**
> **¾ teaspoon salt**
> **½ teaspoon baking soda**
> **⅛ teaspoon ground red pepper, or more to taste (optional)**

Whisk together in another bowl:
> **2 large eggs, lightly beaten**
> **1 cup buttermilk**
> **½ cup grated onions**

Add to the cornmeal mixture and stir just until the dry ingredients are moistened. Pour into a wide skillet—a 10-inch cast-iron skillet works well—and heat to 360°F:
> **1 inch vegetable oil or shortening**

Using a measuring tablespoon, gently drop the batter into the hot fat. Adjust the heat so the batter turns golden brown on one side in about 45 to 60 seconds. Fry several hushpuppies at a time, without crowding, turning them with a slotted spoon, until golden brown on both sides. Transfer to the baking sheet and keep warm in a 200°F oven. Repeat with the remaining batter.

Serve immediately.

Broiled Shrimp with Persillade

Broiled Shrimp or Scallops with Persillade

Persillade is a coating of parsley and garlic, traditionally placed on a rack of lamb. It is also wonderful on broiled seafood.

4 servings

Position the broiler rack about 4 inches from the heat source. Preheat the broiler. Finely chop together by hand or in a small food processor:

**1½ cups fresh breadcrumbs
½ cup fresh parsley leaves
1 clove garlic, peeled
Salt and ground black pepper to taste**

Toss to coat in a shallow roasting pan:

**1½ to 2 pounds sea or bay scallops or large or extra-large shrimp, peeled, deveined if desired, or a combination
2 tablespoons extra-virgin olive oil**

Place under the broiler as close to the heat as possible. Turn the shrimp after the first side becomes pink, 2 minutes or so; turn the scallops when the first side becomes opaque, 2 to 3 minutes. Spread the breadcrumb mixture all over the shellfish, then broil, this time about 4 inches from the heat source, until the breadcrumbs are browned but not burned, 3 to 4 minutes. Serve hot with:

Lemon wedges

Broiled or Grilled Shrimp or Scallops, Basque Style

4 servings

Prepare a medium-hot charcoal fire or preheat a gas grill or broiler. Make sure

the grill rack is clean and place it as close to the heat source as possible. Mix together in a serving bowl:

**½ cup fresh lemon juice
⅓ cup extra-virgin olive oil
1 tablespoon minced garlic
¼ to ½ teaspoon hot red pepper sauce, or to taste
½ cup coarsely chopped fresh herbs (any combination of parsley, sage, thyme, basil, marjoram, oregano, chervil, etc.)
Salt and ground black pepper to taste**

Toss to coat in a shallow bowl:

**1½ to 2 pounds sea scallops or large or extra-large shrimp, peeled, deveined if desired, or a combination
2 tablespoons extra-virgin olive oil**

Place on the grill or under the broiler as close to the heat as possible. Turn the shrimp after the first side becomes pink, 2 minutes or so; turn the scallops when the first side becomes opaque, 2 to 3 minutes. Grill or broil until the second side is pink or opaque; test one of the pieces by cutting into it to make sure it is cooked through. Add the hot shellfish to the herb mixture, toss gently, and serve immediately.

Tomato Concassé

This is a wonderful condiment for grilled chicken or fish. Prepare only as much as you need of this basic preparation, as it does not keep well.

1 cup

Peel, seed, and juice, 17:
2 large ripe tomatoes

Dice the pulp very finely.

Peeling and Deveining Shrimp

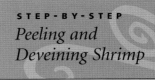

Split the shell on the underside of each shrimp and carefully work the shell loose from the shrimp meat.

Using a small, sharp knife, make a shallow cut down the back of each shrimp to expose the "vein," or intestinal tract.

Catch the vein with the tip of the knife or with your fingers and gently pull it out.

Crabcake and Stewed Tomatoes

Crabcakes

Buy fresh lump crabmeat if you can find it, and give yourself time to refrigerate the cakes after you shape them so that they will hold together better when you cook them.

4 servings

Gently pick over for bits of shell and cartilage:
  1 pound fresh lump crabmeat

In a skillet over medium heat, warm:
  2 tablespoons butter or olive oil

When the butter foam has subsided, add:
  1 tablespoon finely diced red bell peppers (optional)
  ½ cup diced scallions
  1 teaspoon minced garlic

Cook, stirring, until the mixture is tender but not browned, about 10 minutes. Set aside. In a large bowl, mix the crabmeat with:
  1 egg, lightly beaten
  ¼ cup mayonnaise
  1 tablespoon Dijon mustard
  Salt and ground black pepper to taste
  ¼ teaspoon ground red pepper (optional)
  ¼ cup minced fresh parsley, cilantro, or dill
  2 tablespoons fresh breadcrumbs, toasted

Add the sautéed vegetables and blend well. Place on a plate:
  1 to 2 cups fresh breadcrumbs, toasted

Shape the crab mixture into 8 small or 4 large cakes and, 1 at a time, coat each of the cakes in the breadcrumbs, pressing lightly to make sure the crumbs coat evenly. Place the cakes on a rack, or on a plate covered with wax paper, and refrigerate for 1 to 2 hours if you have the time. When you are ready to cook, heat in a large skillet over medium heat:
  ¼ cup butter or oil

When the fat is hot, add the cakes, 1 at a time; do not crowd—it is fine to cook them in two batches. Adjust the heat so that the fat is sizzling but not burning the breadcrumbs. Rotate the cakes from side to side once or twice so that they brown evenly before turning them over after about 5 minutes. Cook until both sides are nicely browned; smaller cakes need a total of 8 to 10 minutes of cooking, larger ones 12 to15 minutes. Keep any finished cakes warm in a 300°F oven while you complete the cooking. Serve hot with:
  Lemon wedges, Aïoli or a seasoned mayonnaise, 121, or Salsa Fresca, 125

Stewed Tomatoes

Stewed tomatoes are a favorite accompaniment to macaroni and cheese and are also good with fish, chicken, and lamb. Since they are juicy, serve stewed tomatoes in separate dishes or small bowls rather than on dinner plates with other foods.

4 servings

Peel, 17:
  8 medium-large very ripe tomatoes (about 3½ pounds)

Cut the tomatoes in half crosswise. Gently squeeze out the seeds and cut out the cores, leaving the tomato halves as intact as possible. Place in a large, heavy saucepan:
  3 to 4 tablespoons unsalted butter or olive oil or a blend of both

Heat over medium heat until the butter melts or the oil becomes fragrant. Add the tomatoes, stir gently to coat with the fat, and cover. Cook, stirring gently from time to time, until the tomatoes

KITCHEN TIP
Blue Crab

Picked crabmeat is probably the most familiar form of crab for most shoppers. It is always worth it to buy the best meat, usually called lump crabmeat, which is made up of the relatively large chunks of meat found in the crab's body. Other grades—claw or flake—do not give as much satisfaction. If possible (and it is possible, especially in the big cities and seafood ports of the East Coast), buy fresh-picked rather than pasteurized crabmeat, for the flavor is noticeably better.

become soft but still retain their shape, 6 to 8 minutes. Season with:
  Salt and ground black pepper to taste
  2 tablespoons minced fresh parsley or finely shredded fresh basil (optional)

If you like, serve with:
  Grated Swiss, Cheddar, or Parmesan cheese

Stewed tomatoes are best when served at once but can be refrigerated in a covered container for up to 3 days. Rewarm over gentle heat.

Deviled Crab

Deviled Crab

4 servings

Preheat the oven to 400°F or turn on the broiler. Pick over and flake:

1½ cups canned or fresh crabmeat

In a large skillet, heat:

2 tablespoons unsalted butter

Add:

¼ cup finely chopped onions
¼ cup finely chopped green bell peppers
¼ cup finely chopped celery

Sauté until the onions are golden. Add:

¼ cup cracker crumbs
¾ cup milk, cream, or clam broth

Cook until thick. Remove from the heat. Beat and add:

2 large eggs
¼ teaspoon salt
1½ teaspoons prepared mustard
A few grains ground red pepper or ⅛ teaspoon hot pepper sauce, or to taste

Add the crabmeat. Pack the mixture into crab shells or ramekins. Brush the tops with:

Melted unsalted butter

Brown in the oven or under the broiler.

Sautéed Cucumbers with Fresh Herbs

Both the expensive shrink-wrapped "gourmet" cucumbers and ordinary garden varieties work well here if you first salt them to draw out their considerable liquid. Tender-skinned garden cucumbers need not be peeled.

4 servings

Scoop out the seeds, then cut crosswise into slices about ⅜ inch thick:

3 large cucumbers or 2 English cucumbers, peeled and halved lengthwise

Sprinkle with:

Salt

Let drain in a colander for at least 15 minutes. Rinse briefly with water, then press out the excess liquid. Melt in a large skillet:

1½ tablespoons butter

Add and cook over medium heat until softened, about 3 minutes:

1 shallot, finely diced (optional)

Add the cucumbers and cook until warm, about 1 minute. Add:

2 to 3 tablespoons water or chicken stock

Reduce the heat and cook until tender but firm, about 4 minutes more. Toss with:

2 teaspoons snipped fresh dill, chives, or chopped parsley
Salt and ground white pepper to taste

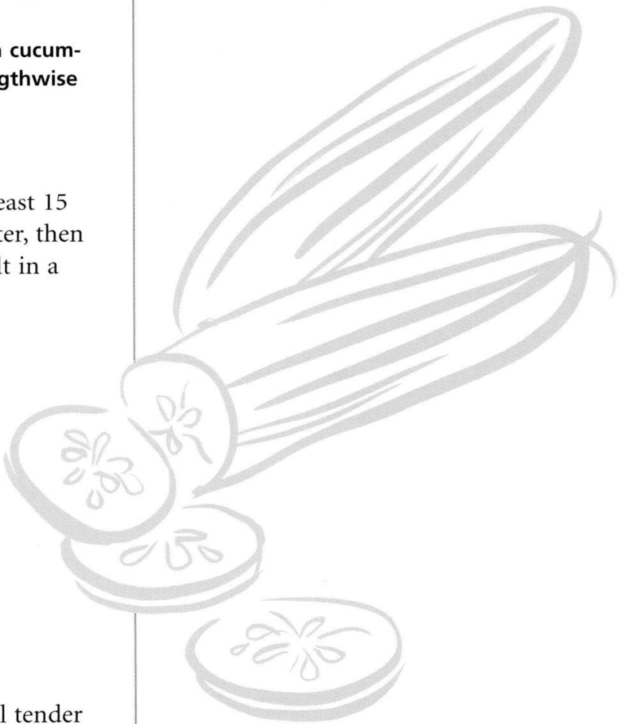

Baked Chicken with Orange Juice

Shopping List

Whole chicken or
    chicken parts

Orange juice

Onion

Butter, preferably
    unsalted

Dark brown sugar

Dijon mustard

Baked Chicken with Orange Juice

A perfect quick after-work dinner.

4 servings

Position a rack in the center of the oven. Preheat the oven to 375°F.

Rinse and pat dry:
1 chicken (about 3 pounds), quartered, or 3 pounds chicken parts

Smear the skin with:
4 teaspoons Dijon mustard

Arrange the chicken skin side down in a shallow roasting pan or baking dish just large enough to hold it in a single layer.

Sprinkle the pieces with:
**½ cup finely chopped onions
2 tablespoons unsalted butter, cut into bits
Salt and ground black pepper to taste**

Pour around the chicken:
1½ cups orange juice

Bake, basting once, for 30 minutes. Turn the chicken skin side up and sprinkle with:
¼ cup firmly packed dark brown sugar

Bake until the chicken is tender and golden, 15 to 20 minutes more. Add more orange juice if the pan seems dry. Remove the chicken to a serving platter. Pour the juices into a small saucepan and boil over high heat until syrupy. Spoon the sauce over the chicken and serve.

Stir-Fry of Napa Cabbage and Carrots

4 servings

Heat a wok or large skillet over high heat. Add and stir-fry for a few seconds, but do not allow the garlic to brown:
**1 tablespoon peanut or vegetable oil
2 cloves garlic, minced
1 tablespoon minced peeled fresh ginger**

Add and stir-fry for 3 minutes:
8 ounces carrots, shredded

Then add and stir-fry until the cabbage is tender, about 3 more minutes:
1 medium-large head Napa cabbage (about 2 pounds), rinsed and thinly sliced

Add and stir well to mix:
**2 tablespoons soy sauce
1 teaspoon toasted sesame oil
½ teaspoon chili paste with garlic or ¼ teaspoon red pepper flakes (optional)**

Serve immediately, sprinkled with:
Minced fresh cilantro or parsley

Chicken and Dumplings

Chicken and Dumplings

4 or 5 servings

Prepare, undercooking the chicken slightly:

Chicken Fricassee, below

Degrease the pan juices and season the fricassee. Push the chicken pieces down so that they are submerged in gravy and drop in spoonfuls over the top:

Dumplings, right

Cover and cook as directed for dumplings.

Serve immediately.

Chicken Fricassee

This delicate and creamy dish of chicken and vegetables has long been an American favorite.

4 or 5 servings

Rinse and pat dry:

3½ to 4½ pounds chicken parts

Separate the legs into thighs and drumsticks; cut each breast half diagonally in half through the bone. If you wish, remove the skin. Sprinkle the chicken with:

Salt and ground black or white pepper to taste

Heat in a heavy 8- to 10-inch skillet over medium heat until fragrant and golden:

4 tablespoons (½ stick) unsalted butter

Place as many chicken pieces in the pan as will fit comfortably and cook, turning once, until pale golden, 3 to 5 minutes on each side. Remove the chicken to a plate and brown the remaining pieces in the same manner. Add to the fat in the pan:

1½ cups chopped onions

Cook, stirring occasionally, until the onions are tender but not browned, about 5 minutes. Stir in:

⅓ cup all-purpose flour

Cook, stirring, for 1 minute, then remove the pan from the heat and whisk in:

2 cups hot water
1¾ cups chicken stock

Whisking constantly, bring the mixture to a boil over high heat. Add:

8 ounces mushrooms, sliced (2⅓ cups)
3 medium carrots, peeled and diced (1 cup)
2 large or 3 medium celery stalks, diced (1 cup)
½ teaspoon dried thyme
1 teaspoon salt
½ teaspoon ground black or white pepper

Return the chicken pieces with all accumulated juices to the pan and bring to a simmer. Reduce the heat so that the liquid barely bubbles. Cover tightly and cook until the dark meat pieces exude clear juices when pricked with a fork, 20 to 30 minutes. Skim off the fat from around the sides of the pan with a spoon. If you wish, stir in:

¼ to ½ cup heavy cream

Season to taste with:

Salt and ground white or black pepper
Several drops of fresh lemon juice

HELPFUL HINT
Making the Fricassee Ahead

The sooner the chicken is served, the juicier it will be. However, the dish can be made ahead. To serve within 1 hour, simply cover the pot and slide to a warm corner of the stove. Otherwise, let the chicken cool to tepid, then cover and refrigerate for up to 3 days. When ready to serve, reheat the fricassee and make the dumplings.

Dumplings

These easy-to-make dumplings are the richest and fluffiest we know.

6 to 8 servings

Mix together:

2 cups all-purpose flour
1 tablespoon baking powder
¾ teaspoon salt

Bring just to a simmer in a small saucepan:

3 tablespoons butter
1 cup milk

Add to the dry ingredients. Stir with a fork or knead by hand 2 to 3 times until the mixture just comes together. Divide the dough into about 18 puffy dumplings. Roll each piece of dough into a rough ball. Gently lay the formed dumplings on the surface of your stew, cover, and simmer for 10 minutes.

Serve immediately.

Baked Stuffed Chicken Breast

Baked Stuffed Boneless Chicken Breasts

6 to 8 servings

Position a rack in the center of the oven. Preheat the oven to 350°F.

Rinse and pat dry:
8 boneless chicken breast halves (about 3 pounds), with or without the skin

Trim any fat around the edges. If you wish, remove the white tendon running through the tenderloins. Place the chicken breasts 1 at a time between sheets of wax paper and gently pound with a mallet or the side of an empty bottle until about ⅜ inch thick. Season with:
Salt and ground black pepper to taste

Heat in a small skillet over medium-high heat until the foam begins to subside:
2 to 3 tablespoons unsalted butter

Add and cook, stirring, until tender but not brown, about 5 minutes:
⅓ cup finely chopped onions

Stir in and cook for 30 seconds:
1 teaspoon minced garlic

Remove the mixture to a bowl and stir in:
2 cups dry unseasoned breadcrumbs
¼ cup grated Parmesan cheese
¼ cup finely chopped fresh parsley
½ teaspoon dried rosemary, crumbled
½ teaspoon dried sage, crumbled
½ teaspoon salt
½ teaspoon ground black pepper

Stir in:
⅓ to ⅔ cup chicken stock

The stuffing should be just moist enough to hold together in a crumbly ball when squeezed firmly in the hand. Do not overmoisten. Taste and adjust the seasonings.

Lightly oil a 13 x 9-inch baking pan. Place ¼ cup stuffing on the center of the underside of each breast and press lightly to compact it. Bring the top and bottom flaps of the chicken up over the stuffing, slightly overlapping the ends, then fold up the sides to enclose the stuffing completely. Lay the packets seam side down in the pan and brush with:
Olive oil

Season with:
Salt and ground black pepper to taste

Bake until the chicken is lightly browned and feels firm when pressed, 20 to 30 minutes. Serve immediately.

Spinach with Currants and Pine Nuts

4 to 6 servings

Wash thoroughly but do not dry:
2 pounds spinach, stemmed

Coarsely chop and place the wet spinach in a large saucepan. Season with:
Salt to taste

Cover and cook over medium heat until the spinach is just wilted, about 5 minutes. Drain well. Heat in a large skillet over medium heat:
¼ cup olive oil

Add:
¼ cup pine nuts

Cook just until they begin to color, about 2 minutes. Add:
2 cloves garlic, finely minced

Cook for another minute. Add the spinach along with:
¼ cup dried currants
Salt and ground black pepper to taste

Cook, stirring frequently, about 5 minutes more.

Serve hot.

Remove any fat from the chicken breast. Remove the tough white tendon, if desired.

Place a chicken breast, underside up, between 2 sheets of wax paper. Pound, starting at the middle.

Place ¼ cup of stuffing on the underside of the chicken breast, compacting the stuffing lightly.

Bring up the top and bottom flaps of the chicken and overlap them over the stuffing. Fold the sides in.

Sautéed Chicken Breast Piccata

Shopping List

Boneless, skinless
   chicken breast halves

Shallots or scallions

Lemon

Butter, preferably
   unsalted

All-purpose flour

Olive oil

Chicken stock

Capers

Sautéed Boneless, Skinless Chicken Breasts Piccata

Sautéed chicken breasts should be a rich nut-brown on the outside, tender and bursting with juice inside.

2 to 4 servings

Rinse and pat dry:
4 boneless, skinless chicken breast halves (about 1½ pounds)

Trim any fat around the edges. If you wish, remove the white tendon running through the tenderloins. Sprinkle both sides with:
Salt and ground black pepper to taste

Spread on a plate:
¼ cup all-purpose flour

Coat the chicken on both sides with the flour, pressing to make the tenderloins, the thin strips of meat on the undersides of the breasts, adhere. Gently shake off the excess flour, holding the chicken tapered side up to avoid detaching the tenderloins. Heat in a heavy 10- to 12-inch skillet over medium-high heat until fragrant and nut-brown:
1½ tablespoons unsalted butter

Add:
1½ tablespoons olive oil

Swirl the butter and oil together. Arrange the chicken tenderloin side down in the skillet and sauté for exactly 4 minutes, keeping the fat as hot as possible without letting it burn. Using tongs, turn the chicken and cook until the flesh feels firm to the touch and milky juices appear around the tenderloins, 3 to 5 minutes more. Keep warm in a 200°F oven.

Remove all but about 1 tablespoon of the fat from the skillet, heat over medium heat, and add:
2 to 3 tablespoons minced shallots or scallions

Cook, stirring, until wilted, about 1 minute. Increase the heat to high and add:
1 cup chicken stock

Bring to a boil, scraping the bottom of the skillet with a wooden spoon to dissolve the browned bits. Add:
3 to 4 tablespoons strained fresh lemon juice
2 tablespoons nonpareil capers, drained

Boil until the mixture is reduced to about ⅓ cup, 3 to 4 minutes. Add any accumulated chicken juices and reduce again. Remove from the heat and swirl in:
2 to 3 tablespoons unsalted butter, softened

Pour the sauce over the chicken and serve immediately.

Smashed Potatoes with Basil Pesto

Smashing or crushing potatoes instead of mashing them has become popular in contemporary American restaurants. Try leaving the peels on some of the potatoes for added texture.

4 to 6 servings

Boil in salted water to cover until very tender:
3 pounds red-skinned or Yellow Finn potatoes

Drain well and return to the pan. Place back on the burner and shake over medium heat to dry the potatoes. Peel all or half the potatoes, then smash with a large spoon or fork, blending in:
½ cup milk
1 tablespoon butter

Add:
½ cup Pesto Sauce, 32
Salt and ground black pepper to taste

Serve hot. The potatoes can be placed in an oiled baking dish and reheated in a 375°F oven just before serving.

Chicken Breast Baked in Parchment

Boneless, Skinless Chicken Breasts Baked in Foil or Parchment with Sun-Dried Tomatoes and Olives

This method of cooking, called in French en papillote, entails baking boneless, skinless chicken breasts in sealed foil packages. The foil traps the juices, resulting in moist and tender meat.

4 servings

Position a rack in the center of the oven. Preheat the oven to 450°F.

Rinse and pat dry:
   4 boneless, skinless chicken breast halves (about 1½ pounds)

Trim any fat around the edges. If you wish, remove the white tendon running through the tenderloins. Season with:
   Salt and ground black pepper to taste

Combine:
   10 Kalamata or other black olives, pitted and finely chopped
   8 sun-dried tomato halves in oil, cut into thin strips
   3 tablespoons sun-dried tomato oil (from the jar of tomatoes) and/or olive oil
   2 tablespoons finely shredded fresh basil or minced fresh parsley

Cut four 12-inch squares of aluminum foil or parchment. Fold each square in half to make a crease at the center. Unfold the foil and lightly oil the shiny side or lightly oil one side of the parchment. Lay each breast on the oiled side of the foil or parchment just to one side of the crease. Spoon the tomato mixture over each breast, leaving a ¼-inch border around the edges. Loosely fold the foil or parchment over the chicken, then crimp the edges of the packet to seal tightly. Place the packets on a baking sheet and bake for 20 minutes. Remove from the oven and let stand for 5 minutes. To avoid being burned by steam, cut a slit in the packets before opening them. If desired, serve with:
   Green Salad, 81

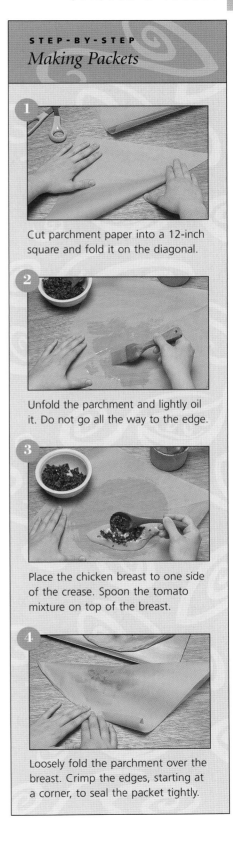

STEP-BY-STEP
Making Packets

1 Cut parchment paper into a 12-inch square and fold it on the diagonal.

2 Unfold the parchment and lightly oil it. Do not go all the way to the edge.

3 Place the chicken breast to one side of the crease. Spoon the tomato mixture on top of the breast.

4 Loosely fold the parchment over the breast. Crimp the edges, starting at a corner, to seal the packet tightly.

Stir-Fried Garlic Chicken

Shopping List

- Boneless, skinless chicken thighs
- Snow peas
- Onion
- Garlic
- Scallions
- Fresh ginger
- Rice or Chinese noodles
- Cornstarch
- Light soy sauce
- Dark soy sauce
- Peanut oil
- Toasted sesame oil
- Chinese cooking wine or dry white wine
- Ketchup
- Chicken stock
- Oyster sauce
- Hoisin sauce

Stir-Fried Garlic Chicken

A tangy dish that comes together very quickly.

2 to 4 servings

BEFORE COOKING:

In a medium bowl, mix together thoroughly:

- **1 tablespoon cornstarch**
- **1 tablespoon Chinese cooking wine or dry white wine**
- **2 teaspoons light soy sauce**
- **2 teaspoons oyster sauce**
- **1 teaspoon salt**
- **1 teaspoon sugar**

Cut into 1½ x ½-inch pieces (this is more easily done if the chicken is partially frozen):

- **1½ pounds boneless, skinless chicken thighs**

Toss in the soy sauce mixture. Cover with plastic wrap and let stand for 20 to 30 minutes. On a small plate, place:

- **4 teaspoons finely minced garlic**
- **1 tablespoon finely minced peeled fresh ginger**

On another small plate, place:

- **20 snow pea pods, trimmed**
- **1 medium onion, cut into ¼-inch-thick slices**

In a small bowl, mix together thoroughly:

- **1 tablespoon hoisin sauce**
- **1 tablespoon ketchup**
- **1 tablespoon toasted sesame oil**
- **1½ teaspoons dark soy sauce**
- **½ teaspoon red pepper flakes**

Have ready:

- **⅔ cup chicken stock**
- **3 scallions, sliced lengthwise into thin strips, then cut into 2-inch sections**

TO COOK:

Heat a wok or large skillet over high heat until hot.

Add:

- **2 tablespoons peanut oil**

Swirl the oil around the pan until very hot but not smoking. Add the minced garlic and ginger and stir briefly until the garlic is very slightly browned. Add the chicken and quickly stir and flip in the oil to separate the pieces. Continue to toss and cook for about 3 minutes. Add the chicken stock and swirl until the stock is heated through. Add the snow peas and onions, stir once, cover, and cook for 2 minutes. Uncover the pan and add the hoisin sauce mixture. Stir lightly until all pieces are thoroughly coated. Sprinkle with the scallions, stir lightly, and remove to a serving dish. Serve immediately with:

- **Hot cooked rice, 123 to 124, or Chinese noodles**

HELPFUL HINT
Stir-Frying

Stir-frying is one of the basic methods of Chinese cooking. It involves three essential elements: the use of very high heat for a brief cooking time; using just enough peanut oil to cook the dish well; and the cutting of all the ingredients to a more or less similar size so that they cook in about the same amount of time. If the cooking times of ingredients are very different although they have been cut to approximately the same size, they may be cooked separately and then combined all at once at the end. In every case, stir-frying involves flipping and stirring the ingredients very rapidly in a wok or skillet. It is always important not to overcook; both the meat and the other ingredients should emerge very hot but full of flavor.

Curried Creamed Chicken

Creamed Chicken or Turkey Using Leftover Meat

This recipe opens the door to a wealth of possibilities using leftovers from the Thanksgiving bird. Serve this on toast, over rice or pasta, or in patty shells.

4 to 6 servings

Melt in a large saucepan over medium-low heat:
   4 tablespoons (½ stick) unsalted butter

Add and whisk until smooth:
   ⅓ cup all-purpose flour

Cook, whisking constantly, for 1 minute. Remove the pan from the heat. Add and whisk until smooth:
   1¾ cups chicken stock
   1¾ cups whole milk, half-and-half, or light cream

Increase the heat to medium and bring the mixture just to a simmer, whisking constantly. Remove the pan from the heat, scrape the corners of the saucepan with a wooden spoon or heatproof rubber spatula, and whisk hard to break up any lumps. Return the pan to the heat and, whisking, bring to a simmer and cook for 1 minute. Stir in:
   4 cups diced or shredded skinless cooked chicken or turkey
   2 to 3 tablespoons sherry (optional)

Cook for 1 minute longer. Remove from the heat and season to taste with:
   Drops of lemon juice
   Salt and ground white and black pepper
   Pinches of freshly grated or ground nutmeg

Creamed Chicken or Turkey Using Canned Soup

This can be served on toast or over rice but is more often used as a base for a pot pie or casserole. In the latter case, simply combine all of the ingredients in a bowl, without heating.

4 to 6 servings

Empty into a large saucepan:
   Two 10¾-ounce cans cream of mushroom or cream of chicken soup

Gradually stir in until smooth:
   1¼ cups whole or low-fat milk

Stir in:
   4 cups diced or shredded skinless cooked chicken or turkey

Bring to a simmer over medium-low heat, stirring constantly, and cook for 1 minute. Remove from the heat and season to taste with:
   Drops of sherry and/or lemon juice
   Ground black or white pepper

Curried Creamed Chicken or Turkey

Because curry has a strong flavor, this dish works well with dark meat as well as white.

4 to 6 servings

Prepare Creamed Chicken or Turkey Using Leftover Meat, left

Add with the flour:
   2 tablespoons mild curry powder
   ½ cup golden raisins

Stir into the finished dish or sprinkle over each serving:
   ¼ cup slivered almonds, toasted

Serve with:
   Hot cooked rice, 123 to 124

Turkey Saltimbocca

Shopping List

Skinless turkey breast cutlets

Prosciutto

Shallots or scallions

Fresh sage

Fresh parsley, if using

Lemon

Butter, preferably unsalted

Olive oil

Plain or smoked mozzarella cheese, if using

Dry white wine

Turkey or chicken stock

Turkey Saltimbocca

Saltimbocca means "jump into the mouth," which is precisely what these delicious stuffed, sauced cutlets do. Prosciutto and sage are the traditional stuffing, but contemporary chefs often add a slice of cheese as well. The Italians make saltimbocca with veal cutlets, but turkey breast is also very good.

4 servings

Rinse and pat dry:
> **8 boneless, skinless turkey breast cutlets (about 1½ pounds)**

Place between sheets of wax paper and gently pound with a mallet or the side of an empty bottle until they are about ¼ inch thick. Season with:
> **Salt and ground black pepper to taste**

Leaving a ¼-inch border around the edges, arrange on half of each cutlet:
> **1 paper-thin slice of prosciutto (about 2 ounces total)**
> **2 large fresh sage leaves (16 total)**

If you wish, cover the prosciutto with:
> **1 thin slice plain or smoked mozzarella cheese (about 4 ounces total)**

Fold the cutlets in half and secure with toothpicks.

Heat in a large, heavy skillet over medium-high heat until fragrant and golden:
> **1 tablespoon olive oil**
> **1 tablespoon unsalted butter**

Add the turkey packages and sauté, turning once, until lightly browned, about 3 minutes each side. Remove to a platter and cover with aluminum foil to keep warm.

Add to the hot pan:
> **2 tablespoons minced shallots or scallions**

Cook, stirring, until wilted, about 1 minute. Pour in:
> **½ cup dry white wine**

Scraping the bottom of the pan with a wooden spoon to loosen the browned bits, boil until the wine is almost evaporated. Add:
> **1 cup turkey or chicken stock**
> **1 tablespoon strained fresh lemon juice**

Boil over high heat until reduced to about ½ cup.

Remove the skillet from the heat and swirl in:
> **2 tablespoons unsalted butter, softened**

Taste and adjust the seasonings, adding a bit more lemon juice, if desired. Pour the sauce over the turkey packages. If you like, sprinkle with:
> **Chopped fresh parsley**

Sautéed Summer Squash with Parsley and Garlic

Give squash plenty of space in a hot skillet so it can sear and brown before giving up its juices. If you find ½-inch-thick baby squashes, just leave them whole.

4 servings

Dice or slice into ½-inch-thick pieces:
> **1½ pounds summer squash**

Heat in a large skillet over high heat:
> **3 tablespoons olive oil**

Drop in the squash a handful at a time, and let each gain a little color before adding the next handful. Sauté until all the squash is golden and tender, about 7 minutes. Remove to a serving dish and toss with:
> **3 tablespoons chopped fresh parsley**
> **2 large cloves garlic, finely chopped**
> **1 teaspoon grated lemon zest (optional)**
> **Salt and ground black pepper to taste**

Turkey Stew with Mushrooms and Marsala

Shopping List

Skinless, boneless turkey thighs	Fresh parsley	Dry or sweet Marsala wine
Mushrooms	Lemon	Balsamic vinegar, if using
Onions	Rice or noodles	Turkey or chicken stock
Garlic	All-purpose flour	
	Olive oil	

Turkey Stew with Mushrooms and Marsala

Boned and skinned chicken thighs work equally well in this simple but delicious recipe.

4 servings

Rinse and pat dry:
1½ pounds boneless turkey thighs (without skin)

Cut the turkey into 1-inch cubes and season with:
Salt and ground black pepper to taste

Heat in a large, heavy skillet over medium-high heat until shimmery:
2 tablespoons olive oil

Add the turkey and brown well on all sides. Remove to a plate. Add to the skillet:
3 cups chopped onions
1 pound mushrooms, quartered through the stem

Cook, stirring, until the onions are lightly browned, 7 to 10 minutes. Add:
2 tablespoons all-purpose flour

Cook, stirring, for 1 minute. Return the turkey with accumulated juices to the skillet and stir in:
2 cups turkey or chicken stock
1 cup dry or sweet Marsala wine
2 tablespoons balsamic vinegar (optional)
1 tablespoon minced garlic

Reduce the heat to low and simmer, uncovered, until the turkey is tender, 10 to 15 minutes. Stir in:
¼ cup chopped fresh parsley
½ to 1 teaspoon grated lemon zest (optional)

Taste and adjust the seasonings.
Serve with:
Hot cooked rice, 123 to 124, or noodles

Golden Pan-Fried Jerusalem Artichokes

4 servings

Heat in a medium skillet until hot:
⅛ to ¼ inch sunflower or olive oil

Add:
1 pound Jerusalem artichokes, scrubbed and cut into ¼-inch-thick rounds

Cook, shaking the pan occasionally, over medium heat until golden, 8 to 10 minutes. Drain on paper towels, then transfer to a serving dish and toss with:
Salt and ground black pepper to taste
Minced fresh parsley, dill, or tarragon

Serve with:
Lemon wedges

Scrub the Jerusalem artichokes well with a vegetable brush, being sure to get into every nook and cranny.

Using a stainless steel knife, slice the Jerusalem artichokes and drop the slices into a bowl of lemon water to prevent discoloration.

Ground Turkey Loaf

Ground Turkey or Chicken Loaf

You can cook this delicious mixture as a loaf, as burgers, or as meatballs.

4 servings

Position a rack in the center of the oven. Preheat the oven to 350°F. Lightly oil a 4- to 5-cup loaf pan.

Heat in a medium skillet over medium heat until fragrant:
   1 tablespoon olive oil

Add:
   ½ cup chopped onions
   1 clove garlic, minced

Cook, stirring, until the onions are tender but not browned, 5 to 7 minutes. Remove to a medium bowl and add:
   1 pound ground turkey or chicken
   1 large egg
   ¼ cup grated Parmesan cheese
   2 tablespoons milk
   2 tablespoons dry unseasoned breadcrumbs
   1 tablespoon tomato paste
   1 tablespoon chopped fresh basil, or 1 teaspoon dried
   1 tablespoon chopped fresh parsley, or 1 teaspoon dried
   1½ teaspoons salt
   ½ teaspoon ground black pepper

Thoroughly combine the mixture, then pat into the prepared pan. Bake until the center feels firm when pressed, about 35 minutes. Let stand for 10 minutes, then unmold from the pan if you wish. Serve hot.

If desired, serve with mashed potatoes.

Braised Carrots

4 servings

Place in a sauté pan that has a lid and is wide enough to hold the carrots in a single layer:
   1 pound carrots, peeled, quartered lengthwise, and cut into even sticks
   ½ cup water or chicken or beef stock
   1½ tablespoons butter
   1 teaspoon sugar or brown sugar
   ½ teaspoon salt

Simmer, covered, over medium heat until the carrots are tender and most of the liquid has been absorbed, 15 to 20 minutes. When the pan is almost dry, continue to cook the carrots for a few minutes more, then season with:
   1 tablespoon chopped fresh parsley, chervil, tarragon, or thyme
   Ground black pepper to taste

Or top with:
   Grated Gruyère or Parmesan cheese

Pan Gravy for Turkey Loaf

A roux-thickened sauce. This recipe may be doubled.

About 2 cups

Place a skillet over medium heat and pour in:
   2 to 4 tablespoons reserved fat from the loaf pan, melted butter, or rendered bacon fat

Stir in:
   2 to 4 tablespoons all-purpose flour

Cook, whisking or stirring constantly for several minutes to remove the raw taste of the flour and smooth the mixture. Add any remaining pan juices and:
   Enough chicken stock or other liquid to make 2 cups
   ¼ cup or more light or heavy cream (optional)
   Salt and ground black pepper to taste

Cook, whisking or stirring, until the gravy is thickened to the desired consistency. Strain through a fine-mesh sieve, if desired, and serve hot.

Steak Diane

Steak Diane

This recipe also works nicely with medallions of pork.

4 servings

Pat dry:
4 boneless beef steaks (6 to 8 ounces each), ¾ to 1¼ inches thick

Season both sides with:
Salt and ground black pepper to taste

Heat in a large, heavy skillet over medium-high heat:
1 tablespoon olive oil

Put the steaks into the pan and sauté for about 5 minutes each side for medium-rare, less time for rare or more for medium. Make a small incision and check the center. It should be slightly less done than desired, for it will continue to cook somewhat off the heat. Remove the steaks to a warmed platter. Pour off any fat in the pan. Return the pan to medium-high heat. Add and heat until hot:
2 tablespoons butter

Add and cook, shaking the pan, until softened, about 2 minutes:
½ cup chopped shallots or scallions (white part only)

Stir in:
¼ cup beef stock
¼ cup brandy
1 tablespoon Dijon mustard
2 teaspoons fresh lemon juice
1 teaspoon Worcestershire sauce
Salt and ground black pepper to taste

Boil for 1 to 2 minutes, scraping up any browned bits. Add any juices from the steaks. If desired, remove from the heat and add, swirling the pan until melted:
2 tablespoons butter, softened

Garnish with:
2 tablespoons snipped fresh chives
2 tablespoons chopped fresh parsley

Pour the sauce over the steaks and serve immediately.

Sautéed Steak with Red Wine Herb Sauce

Ideal for boneless top loin, tenderloin, or top sirloin cap steaks.

4 servings

Pat dry:
4 boneless beef steaks (6 to 8 ounces each), ¾ to 1¼ inches thick

Season both sides with:
Salt and ground black pepper to taste

Heat in a large, heavy skillet over medium-high heat:
1 tablespoon olive oil

Put the steaks in the pan and sauté for about 5 minutes each side for medium-rare, less time for rare or more for medium. Make a small incision and check the center. It should be slightly less done than desired, for it will continue to cook somewhat off the heat. Remove the steaks to a warmed platter. Pour off all but 1 tablespoon of fat from the pan and place the pan over medium-high heat. Add:
2 tablespoons chopped shallots

Cook for 1 minute. Add:
½ cup each dry red wine and chicken or beef stock
1 teaspoon chopped fresh rosemary or scant ½ teaspoon dried

Increase the heat to high and boil the sauce, scraping up any browned bits, until it is reduced to about ¼ cup. Add any accumulated juices from the steaks. For a richer sauce, swirl in, off the heat:
1 tablespoon butter

Season with:
Salt and ground black pepper to taste

Serve immediately.

Green Salad

4 to 6 servings

Combine in a salad bowl:
2 large heads Boston or Bibb lettuce, washed, dried, and torn into bite-sized pieces
1 tablespoon chopped fresh parsley (optional)
1 tablespoon snipped fresh chives (optional)

Toss well to coat with:
½ to ¾ cup Basic Vinaigrette, 119, or one of the variations

Serve immediately.

Pan-Seared Steak with Smoky Onions

Pan-Seared Top Round Steak with Smoky Onions and Red Wine

*T*his bold recipe turns a little-appreciated cut of beef into a first-class main course. The smoky flavor of the onions marries beautifully with the flavors of the steak and red wine. The high heat of the pan puts out a good amount of smoke, so be sure your kitchen exhaust fan is working.

4 to 6 servings

Pat dry:
> **1 beef top round steak (1½ to 2 pounds), 1½ inches thick**

Rub all sides of the meat with:
> **2 tablespoons cracked black peppercorns**
> **1 tablespoon salt**

Heat a large, heavy skillet, preferably cast iron, over high heat until quite hot. To determine when the pan is hot enough, touch a corner of the steak to the pan; it should sizzle briskly. Once the pan is hot, sear the steak about 6 minutes on each side. Make a small incision and check the center. It should be slightly less done than desired, for it will continue to cook somewhat off the heat. Remove the steak from the pan and let it stand, loosely covered. Heat the pan over medium-high heat.

Add:
> **3 medium, red onions, halved and thinly sliced**

Cook, stirring constantly, until well colored, 2 to 3 minutes. Expect the onions to look somewhat scorched; this is what gives the dish its smoky flavor. Add:
> **1½ cups dry red wine**

Boil until reduced by half, 3 to 4 minutes. Remove from the heat and stir in:
> **4 tablespoons (½ stick) cold butter, cut into pieces**

Once the butter is no longer visible, add:
> **⅓ cup chopped fresh parsley**
> **Salt and ground black pepper to taste**

Very thinly slice the steak across the grain and spoon the onion sauce on top.

If desired, serve with roasted root vegetables.

Basic Pan-Broiled Steak

*P*an-broiled steaks tend to smoke, so turn the exhaust fan on high or open the windows.

4 servings

Pat dry:
> **4 small beef steaks (2 to 12 ounces each) or 2 larger steaks (¾ to 1½ pounds each), ¾ to 1½ inches thick**

If the meat is very lean, brush it with:
> **Olive oil**

Season both sides of the steaks with:
> **Salt and ground black pepper to taste**

Heat a large, heavy skillet or griddle over medium-high heat. You may need 2 skillets if the steaks are large. To determine when the pan is hot enough, touch a corner of the steak to the pan; it should sizzle briskly. Once the pan is hot, sear the steaks on one side, without crowding, for about 5 minutes. Turn them over and sear the other side for 3 to 4 minutes for rare, 5 to 8 minutes for medium. You may need to turn the

steak more than once if one side gets too brown before the steak is done. Pour off any fat that accumulates during cooking.

Serve immediately with:
> **Flavored Butter, 122, or one of the variations**

KITCHEN TIP
Pan-Broiling Steak

Pan-broiling, or dry-skillet cooking, is a simple and convenient method for cooking any steak up to 2 inches thick. It is especially useful for steaks less than 1 inch thick, which fare poorly if grilled or broiled. As an added advantage, pan-broiling is an excellent method for achieving a good crisp crust.

Pan-broiling is best done in a well-seasoned heavy skillet or griddle or nonstick skillet. Steaks should be patted dry and seasoned well with salt, pepper, and other spices immediately before cooking; salting too far in advance makes the surface too moist for the meat to brown evenly. It is important to get the pan hot enough that the meat sizzles the instant it hits the pan; lower temperatures will not produce the desired crust. Do not overcrowd the pan, and cook the steaks uncovered, turning them occasionally. Pour off any fat that accumulates to keep from frying the steaks.

Beef and Vegetable Stir-Fry

Shopping List

Beef steak	Scallions	Peanut oil
Red and green bell peppers	Fresh ginger	Toasted sesame oil
	Fresh cilantro, if using	Dry sherry or Chinese rice wine
Mushrooms, preferably shiitake	Rice or Chinese noodles	Chicken stock, if using
Snow peas		Chili oil, if using
Onion	Cornstarch	Fermented black beans, if using
Garlic	Soy sauce	

Beef and Vegetable Stir-Fry

Stir-frying is the Chinese technique of using a little oil and an Asian flavor base to cook meat, fish, and vegetables. This method is quick and easy; a Chinese wok is handy, but a large skillet will also do. This is a basic recipe and can be varied with different combinations of vegetables and seasonings. Any cut of lean, tender beef, such as flank steak, sirloin steak, sirloin tip, skirt steak, or top sirloin cap steak, can be used. Lean pork, lamb, or chicken can be substituted for the beef.

4 to 6 servings

BEFORE COOKING:

Mix in a medium bowl:
- **¼ cup soy sauce**
- **2 tablespoons dry sherry or Chinese rice wine**
- **1 tablespoon water**
- **1 tablespoon sugar**
- **1 tablespoon cornstarch**
- **2 teaspoons toasted sesame oil**

Add and toss to coat:
- **1 pound beef steak, sliced across the grain into 2 x ½-inch strips**

Marinate the beef for at least 20 minutes.

On a large platter, place in separate piles:
- **1 medium onion, chopped**
- **2 bell peppers, preferably 1 green and 1 red, chopped**
- **1 cup mushrooms, preferably shiitake, wiped clean, stemmed, and cut into ½-inch strips**
- **4 scallions, cut into 2-inch lengths**
- **1 cup snow peas, trimmed, cooked for 30 seconds in boiling water, rinsed, and drained**

Combine in a small bowl:
- **2 tablespoons minced peeled fresh ginger**
- **1 tablespoon minced garlic**

- **⅓ to 1 teaspoon chili oil, or more to taste (optional)**

Have ready:
- **2 to 4 tablespoons chopped fresh cilantro or chopped scallions**
- **1 tablespoon fermented black beans, rinsed, drained, and chopped (optional)**
- **1½ teaspoons red pepper flakes, or more to taste (optional)**

Remove the beef from the marinade. Add to the marinade and set aside:
- **⅓ cup chicken stock or water**

TO COOK:

Heat in a wok or large, heavy skillet over very high heat until hot but not smoking:
- **2 tablespoons peanut oil**

Add the ginger mixture and stir-fry until fragrant but not browned, about 30 seconds. Add the beef and cook, quickly stirring and flipping it in the oil to separate the slices, until browned, about 2 minutes. Remove and reserve the beef, ginger, and garlic.

Heat the wok or skillet over high heat until hot. Add:
- **1 tablespoon peanut oil**

Heat until hot but not smoking. Add the onion, peppers, and mushrooms and stir-fry until crisp-tender, about 2 minutes. Add the 2-inch scallion pieces, the snow peas, and the Chinese black beans and red pepper flakes, if using. Return the meat to the pan along with any accumulated juices and the marinade mixture. Toss for 10 seconds over high heat. Serve with:
- **Hot cooked rice, 123 to 124, or Chinese noodles**

Garnish with the cilantro or scallions.

STEP-BY-STEP

Preparing Shiitake Mushrooms

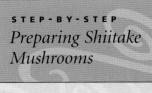

Wipe the shiitake mushrooms clean. Cut away the stems close to the base of the caps.

Slice the mushroom caps into ½-inch-wide strips. Save the tough stems to simmer in stock.

Stir-Fried Beef with Asparagus

Stir-Fried Beef with Asparagus

Both the beef and the vegetable take on rich flavor in this popular dish.

4 to 6 servings

BEFORE COOKING:

Mix well in a medium bowl:
- **2 tablespoons Chinese cooking wine or dry white wine**
- **2 tablespoons oyster sauce**
- **1 tablespoon cornstarch**
- **2 teaspoons light soy sauce**
- **1½ teaspoons salt**
- **1½ teaspoons sugar**

Cut across the grain to make very thin 2 x 1-inch slices (this is more easily done if the meat is partially frozen):
- **1 pound flank steak**

Add the meat to the soy mixture, cover with plastic wrap, and marinate for at least 30 minutes.

Place in cold water to cover:
- **1½ pounds medium-thick asparagus, trimmed and cut into 1-inch pieces**

Place on a small plate:
- **2½ tablespoons fermented black beans, rinsed lightly under cold water and mashed to a paste**
- **1 tablespoon finely minced garlic**
- **1 teaspoon red pepper flakes (optional)**

Mix well in a small bowl:
- **¾ cup chicken stock**
- **½ teaspoon salt**
- **½ teaspoon sugar**

Mix well in a cup:
- **2 tablespoons cornstarch**
- **3 tablespoons cool water, leaving mixing spoon in for later**

Have ready:
- **1 tablespoon toasted sesame oil**

TO COOK:

Heat a wok or large, heavy skillet over high heat. Add and heat until very hot but not smoking:
- **2 tablespoons peanut oil**

Add the beef and cook, quickly stirring and flipping it in the oil to separate the slices, until browned, about 2 minutes. Drain in a strainer or colander.

Heat the wok or skillet over high heat until hot. Add:
- **2 tablespoons peanut oil**

Heat until very hot but not smoking. Add the black beans, garlic, and pepper flakes. Briefly cook, stirring, until the garlic browns very slightly.

Drain the asparagus, add it to the wok, and cook for 2 minutes. Stir in the chicken stock mixture and bring to a boil. Cook the asparagus for 1 to 2 minutes more, depending on thickness.

Return the beef to the wok or skillet. Stir and toss quickly to mix completely.

Stir the cornstarch mixture, then pour it gradually into the sauce while stirring. Cook, stirring, until the sauce is thickened. Add the sesame oil, give a final stir, and serve immediately with:
- **Hot cooked rice, 123 to 124, or Chinese noodles**

Hot cooked rice, 123 to 124

STEP-BY-STEP

Preparing Flank Steak and Asparagus for Stir-Fry

Place partially frozen flank steak on a cutting board. Using a long, thin-bladed knife, cut across the grain into very thin slices. Cut each slice into 2 x 1-inch pieces.

Hold a rinsed spear of asparagus with one hand near the base of the spear and the other hand farther toward the tip. Bend until the spear breaks where it begins to toughen.

Cut each spear into 1-inch bite-sized pieces, preferably on the diagonal.

Beef Stroganoff and Sautéed Mushrooms

Shopping List

Beef tenderloin, top loin, or sirloin tip	Butter, preferably unsalted	Olive oil or vegetable oil, if using
Mushrooms	Sour cream	Dijon mustard
Onion	Rice or egg noodles	Beef stock
Garlic	All-purpose flour	
Fresh parsley		

Beef Stroganoff

The enduring appeal of this dish lies in its simplicity. Since its origin in Russia in the 18th century, there have been many variations on the theme of sautéed beef slices in a cream-based sauce. Some recipes include onions and mushrooms, and others spice the sauce with mustard. In our version, the beef is cooked with onions for flavor, but then the onions are discarded so as not to interfere with the taste of slices of tender beef in a simple roux-thickened cream sauce. Sautéed mushrooms and rice pilaf are good side dishes. Stroganoff is an elegant way to use up any leftover tenderloin pieces cut from the whole filet.

4 to 6 servings

Cut into thin 2 x ¼-inch strips:
1½ pounds beef tenderloin, top loin, or sirloin tip, well trimmed

Season with:
Salt and ground black pepper to taste

Melt in a small saucepan over medium heat:
1½ tablespoons butter

Add and stir with a whisk until smooth:
1 tablespoon all-purpose flour

Add and whisk constantly for 3 to 4 minutes to prevent lumps:
1 cup beef stock, heated to a simmer

Simmer until the sauce is smooth and thickened. Set aside and keep warm. Heat in a large skillet over medium-high heat:
2 tablespoons butter

Add the beef along with:
1 onion, thinly sliced

Cook quickly, shaking the pan and stirring, until evenly browned, 1 to 2 minutes. The meat should remain pink in the center. Remove the meat to a warmed platter with a slotted spoon and discard the onion. Return the sauce to medium heat, stir in, and heat briefly without boiling:
3 tablespoons sour cream
1 teaspoon Dijon mustard
Salt and ground black pepper to taste

Add any accumulated juices from the cooked meat. Spoon the sauce over the meat and serve immediately with:
Egg Noodles, 38 to 39, or
Basic Pilaf, 124
Sautéed Mushrooms, right

Sautéed Mushrooms

Use a large skillet and give the mushrooms plenty of room so that they will brown instead of steam in their own juices. These are great over steak or grilled fish, stirred into 2 cups cooked pasta or rice, or used as an omelet filling.

2 or 3 servings

Heat in a very large skillet over high heat:
2½ to 3 tablespoons butter or olive or vegetable oil, or a combination

Add:
1 pound any variety or combination of mushrooms, wiped clean and sliced

Cook, tossing constantly, until the mushrooms begin to color, 5 to 7 minutes. Add:
¼ to ⅓ cup chopped fresh parsley
2 to 3 cloves garlic, chopped

Cook for 1 minute more. Season with:
Salt and ground black pepper to taste

Serve immediately.

Sautéed Pork Chop with Pan Sauce

Sautéed Pork Chops with Herb Pan Sauce

The technique of first sautéing over high heat to give the meat a crust and then finishing by covering the pan and reducing the heat works best for all pork chops 1 inch thick, cut from the loin.

4 servings

Pat dry:
4 center-cut pork loin chops (bone-in or boneless), 1 inch thick

Season with:
Salt and ground black pepper to taste

Heat in a large skillet over high heat:
1½ teaspoons unsalted butter
1½ teaspoons olive or vegetable oil

Brown the chops 1 minute on each side. Reduce the heat to low, cover the pan, and cook the chops for 5 minutes, 4 minutes if boneless. Turn the chops over, cover the pan again, and cook for 5 minutes more, 4 minutes if boneless. They will be well browned on the outside and slightly pink in the center. Remove to a warmed platter or plates. Pour off the fat and heat the skillet over medium-high heat. Add:
⅓ cup chicken stock, apple cider, wine, or other liquid

Stir with a wooden spoon to loosen and dissolve any browned bits, bring to a boil, and add:
¼ cup minced shallots
1 bay leaf
2 teaspoons Dijon mustard (optional)
1½ teaspoons fresh lemon juice, white wine vinegar, or Cognac, or to taste
Salt and ground black pepper to taste

Cook, stirring occasionally, over medium-high heat until slightly thickened, 1 to 2 minutes. Add and cook until reduced by about half, 3 to 5 minutes:
¼ cup heavy cream (optional)

Remove the pan from the heat. Strain the sauce through a fine-mesh sieve, if desired, and stir in:
1 tablespoon minced fresh herbs (parsley, thyme, and/or rosemary)

Swirl in:
1 tablespoon butter, preferably unsalted, softened (optional)

Arrange the chops on plates, spoon the sauce over, and just before serving, garnish with:
Fresh herb sprigs (optional)

Spanish Rice

This rice is delicious served with chicken or pork and, because it is oven baked, is a foolproof rice dish for any occasion.

4 to 6 servings

Preheat the oven to 350°F.

Combine in an ovenproof skillet or casserole:
2 slices bacon, minced
½ cup chopped onions
½ cup chopped green bell peppers
1 clove garlic, minced

Cook, stirring, over medium heat until the onions are golden, about 5 minutes. Add:
1 cup long-grain white rice

Stir until well coated. Add:
1¾ cups chicken stock
1 cup chopped drained canned tomatoes
½ teaspoon sweet or hot paprika
¼ teaspoon ground black pepper

Bring to a boil. Stir once, cover, and bake until the stock is absorbed and the rice is tender, about 25 minutes. Uncover and let stand for 5 minutes before serving.

STEP-BY-STEP
Making a Pan Sauce

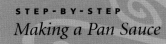

Heat the degreased pan over medium-high heat and pour in stock, cider, or wine. Scrape the bottom to deglaze, and bring to a boil.

Add shallots, bay leaf, mustard, Cognac, and salt and pepper and stir until thickened, 1 to 2 minutes. If using cream, add and cook until reduced by half.

Remove from the heat and discard the bay leaf or strain the sauce. Stir in the fresh herbs, then swirl in the butter.

Sautéed Veal on Arugula Salad

Sautéed Veal Medallions on Arugula Tomato Salad

4 servings

Whisk together in a small bowl:
- ¼ cup extra-virgin olive oil
- 2 tablespoons fresh orange juice
- 2 tablespoons fresh lemon juice
- 1 teaspoon grated orange zest
- Salt and ground black pepper to taste

Toss together in a large bowl:
- 6 cups torn arugula leaves
- 2 medium tomatoes, cored and diced

Position a rack in the lower third of the oven. Preheat the oven to 180°F. Have ready an ovenproof platter. Pat dry:
- 8 veal medallions, cut ¾ inch thick from the center loin

Season with:
- Salt and ground black pepper to taste

Heat in a large skillet over medium-high heat:
- 2 tablespoons unsalted butter

Add the medallions in batches, being careful not to crowd the pan, and sear until golden on the bottom, about 2 minutes. Turn and sear the second side. Remove to the platter and keep warm in the oven. Repeat, adding more butter to the pan as needed, until all the medallions are cooked. Thinly slice the meat when cooked. Toss the arugula with the orange dressing and arrange the salad on 4 plates. Divide the veal and arrange it over the salads. Sprinkle with:
- Salt and ground black pepper to taste

Serve immediately.

Sautéed Veal Medallions

4 servings

Position a rack in the lower third of the oven. Preheat the oven to 180°F. Have ready an ovenproof platter.

Pat dry:
- 8 veal medallions, cut ¾ inch thick from the center loin

Season with:
- Salt and ground black pepper to taste

Heat in a large skillet over medium-high heat:
- 2 tablespoons unsalted butter

Add the medallions in batches, being careful not to crowd the pan, and sear until golden on the bottom, about 2 minutes. Turn and sear the second side. Remove to the platter and keep warm in the oven. Repeat, adding more butter to the pan as needed, until all the medallions are cooked. Increase the heat to high and add to the skillet:
- ¼ cup chicken or veal stock

Boil, stirring, until the sauce is syrupy and glazelike, 1 to 2 minutes. Spoon the sauce over the medallions and serve.

Creamed Cabbage

The cream mingles with water from the cabbage, resulting in a thin but very flavorful sauce.

4 servings

Bring to a rolling boil in a stockpot:
- 16 cups (4 quarts) water
- 1½ tablespoons salt

Remove the outer leaves from:
- 1 pound green cabbage, preferably Savoy

Cut into quarters, remove the core, and cut crosswise into thin slices. Cook, uncovered, for 3 minutes, then drain and press out the excess water. Melt in a large skillet:
- 2 tablespoons butter

Add the cabbage along with:
- ½ cup crème fraîche or heavy cream
- 1 tablespoon snipped fresh dill,
- 1 teaspoon caraway seeds, or
- 10 juniper berries
- 1 teaspoon salt
- Ground black pepper to taste

Toss well, then simmer until the cabbage is tender but not mushy, about 15 minutes. Season to taste with:
- Several drops dry sherry or red wine vinegar
- Salt to taste

Veal Marsala

Veal Scaloppine

Serve simply, as in this recipe, or try with any of the variations.

4 servings

Preheat the oven to 180°F. Have ready an ovenproof platter.

Have ready:
1 pound veal scaloppine slices (8 to 12), cut a little more than ¼ inch thick and pounded to slightly less than ¼ inch thick

Season with:
Salt and ground black pepper to taste

Dredge in:
½ cup all-purpose flour

Shake off the excess. Heat in a large skillet over high heat:
1 tablespoon olive oil
1 tablespoon unsalted butter

Cook the scaloppine in batches, being careful not to crowd the pan. Brown quickly, 30 to 60 seconds each side. Remove to the platter and keep warm in the oven. Repeat, adding more oil and butter to the pan as needed, until all the scaloppine are cooked. Season with:
Salt and ground black pepper to taste

Serve immediately.

Veal Marsala

Although many variations of this classic dish include mushrooms, this traditional recipe does not.

Prepare Veal Scaloppine, left, without placing the veal in the oven after browning. After the scaloppine have been cooked, set them aside and add ⅔ cup dry Marsala wine to the pan. Bring to a boil, scraping up the browned bits with a wooden spoon. Reduce the heat and simmer until cooked down to about ½ cup. Whisk in 2 tablespoons softened unsalted butter. Continue to simmer until the sauce becomes thicker and velvety. Return the veal to the pan along with 2 tablespoons chopped fresh parsley and simmer the meat in the sauce so that it warms through, about 1 minute. Remove from the heat and serve immediately with pasta and a green vegetable.

Veal Piccata

Prepare Veal Scaloppine, left, and keep warm in the oven. Add ¼ cup dry white wine and ⅓ cup fresh lemon juice to the pan. Bring to a boil, scraping up the browned bits with a wooden spoon. Reduce the heat and simmer until slightly reduced, about 5 minutes. Turn off the heat and quickly whisk in 4 tablespoons softened unsalted butter. Season to taste with salt and pepper and 2 tablespoons chopped fresh parsley. Spoon the sauce over the scaloppine and serve immediately.

Grilled Lamb Chops

Broiled or Grilled Lamb Chops

*M*ake sure the chops are close enough to the heat to brown well but not so close that they char; 3 to 4 inches is usually ideal.

4 servings

Preheat the broiler and broiler pan or prepare a medium-hot charcoal fire.

Pat dry:
   8 lamb chops, preferably from the rib or loin, about 1 inch thick

Rub both sides with:
   2 tablespoons olive oil
   1 teaspoon salt
   ½ teaspoon ground black pepper

Place the chops on the broiler pan or grill rack and cook for 4½ to 5 minutes each side for medium-rare. Cook the chops for 1 minute more for medium. Remove the chops to a warmed platter or plates and serve immediately. If desired, serve with a baked potato and:
   Anchovy Butter, 122

Pan-Broiled Lamb Chops

A method using no fat and higher heat.

4 servings

Pat dry:
   8 lamb chops, preferably from the rib or loin, about 1 inch thick

Season with:
   1 teaspoon salt
   ½ teaspoon ground black pepper

Heat a well-seasoned cast-iron or non-stick skillet over high heat. Add the chops and cook for 3½ to 4 minutes each side. Remove the chops to a warmed platter or plates and serve immediately. If desired, serve with:
   Flavored Butter, 122, or one of the variations, or chopped fresh parsley

---

KITCHEN TIP
Lamb Chops

The most popular, but expensive, lamb chops are loin and rib chops, prized for their tenderness and good-sized nugget of eye meat. Rib chops are recognizable by the "handle" of rib bone extending from the eye. Loin chops are more compact and somewhat meatier, resembling a tiny T-bone steak. Either can be grilled, broiled, pan-broiled, or sautéed. Chops at least ¾ inch thick are best, as thinner ones are easy to overcook. Depending on the size of the chops, figure on 2 or 3 chops per person.

Roasted Asparagus

*I*t is surprising how delicious these delicate spears can be when roasted in a very hot oven.

4 servings

Preheat the oven to 500°F.

Snap off the bottoms and peel the lower halves of:
   1 pound asparagus

Arrange the spears in a single layer in a shallow baking dish and drizzle over them very lightly:
   Extra-virgin olive oil

Toss the spears to coat lightly. Roast until tender but still slightly firm, 8 to 10 minutes. Sprinkle with:
   Salt and ground black pepper to taste
   Extra-virgin olive oil
   2 tablespoons minced fresh parsley, tarragon, and/or chives

Serve as a first course at room temperature, garnished with:
   Lemon wedges

Venetian-Style Liver and Onions

Liver and Onions

This is one of the tastiest and most traditional of all calf's liver dishes. The essential element in this recipe is the long, slow cooking of the onions to bring out their natural sugars.

4 to 6 servings

Heat in a large skillet with a lid or in a Dutch oven over medium-low heat:
> **3 tablespoons olive oil**

Add:
> **3 to 4 large onions (1½ to 2 pounds), halved and thinly sliced**
> **Generous sprinkling of salt and ground black pepper**

Cover the pan and cook, stirring often, over low heat until the onions are very soft but not colored, 20 to 30 minutes. Meanwhile, remove the membrane from and cut into ½-inch slices:
> **1½ pounds calf's liver**

Season all sides with:
> **Salt and ground black pepper to taste**

Dredge in:
> **All-purpose flour**

Shake off the excess four. Heat in a large skillet over medium-high heat:
> **¼ cup olive oil**

Add the liver in batches and sauté for 2 to 3 minutes each side. Remove the liver to a warmed platter as it becomes done. Spoon the cooked onions over the liver and serve immediately.

Venetian-Style Liver and Onions

4 to 6 servings

Heat in a large skillet with a lid or in a Dutch oven over medium-low heat:
> **3 tablespoons olive oil**

Add:
> **3 to 4 large onions (1½ to 2 pounds), halved and thinly sliced**
> **Generous sprinkling of salt and ground black pepper**

Cover the pan and cook, stirring often, over low heat until the onions are very soft but not colored, 20 to 30 minutes. Meanwhile, remove the membrane from and cut into ½-inch-thick slices:
> **1½ pounds calf's liver**

Season all sides with:
> **Salt and ground black pepper to taste**

Dredge in:
> **All-purpose flour**

Shake off the excess flour. Heat in a large skillet over medium-high heat:
> **¼ cup olive oil**

Sauté the liver in batches for 1 to 2 minutes each side. Pour into the skillet over high heat:
> **⅓ cup balsamic vinegar or ⅓ cup red wine vinegar and a pinch of sugar**

Boil, scraping up the browned bits on the bottom of the pan, until the vinegar is reduced to 3 to 4 tablespoons. To serve, spoon the onions over the liver and sprinkle with the vinegar. If desired, serve with:
> **Hot Cooked Rice, 123 to 124**

KITCHEN TIP
Preparing Liver

If your butcher has not done so, remove the outer membrane on the slices of liver. Make ⅛-inch cuts at 1-inch intervals around the outside of the slices. Liver has a tendency to shrink and curl when it is cooked; these cuts will help keep the pieces flat.

Tacos Filled with Ground Beef

Tacos Filled with Ground Beef, Turkey, or Chicken

Tacos are simply food wrapped in tortillas. Until recently, the tacos we saw in the United States were thin, crackly, machine-made tortilla folders filled with ground beef, grated cheese, lettuce, and perhaps some salsa. In fact, though, the tortillas for tacos can be folded or rolled around the filling, and they can be served soft or fried either before or after they have been filled. The range of possible fillings is as wide as the range of American sandwich fixings.

4 servings

Have ready:
12 corn tortillas

Wrap the tortillas in a dishtowel, place in a steamer over simmering water, cover, and steam for 1 minute. Turn off the heat and let stand in the covered steamer for 20 minutes. Meanwhile, heat in a medium skillet over medium heat until hot but not smoking:
2 tablespoons vegetable oil

Add:
½ medium red onion, minced

Cook, stirring often, until softened, 4 to 5 minutes. Increase the heat to medium-high and add:
1 pound ground beef, turkey, or chicken

Cook, breaking up the meat with a wooden spoon, until no longer pink, about 3 minutes. Stir in:
1 to 3 cloves garlic, minced
1 tablespoon chili powder
2 teaspoons ground cumin
2 teaspoons ground coriander
Pinch of anise seeds, lightly crushed
  (optional)
Salt to taste

Cook, stirring, for 30 seconds. Add:
1 cup tomato sauce
Minced fresh jalapeños or other chili
  peppers or hot red pepper sauce
  to taste

Cook, stirring occasionally, over low heat for 10 minutes. Meanwhile, place on the serving table in separate bowls or on a large platter:
2 cups shredded romaine lettuce,
  washed and dried
4 ounces queso fresco or Monterey Jack
  cheese, shredded
Salsa Fresca, 125
Corn, Cherry Tomato, and Avocado
  Salsa, right

If necessary, reheat the meat mixture and transfer to a serving bowl. Place the warmed tortillas in a basket and serve immediately, allowing each guest to layer ingredients into his or her own taco as desired. Or layer each tortilla with the ground meat mixture, lettuce, cheese, and a generous dollop of one of the salsas, fold over, and serve 3 to each guest.

Corn, Cherry Tomato, and Avocado Salsa

About 2 cups

Boil in salted water to cover for 1 minute, drain, and remove the kernels from:
2 ears sweet corn, husked and silk
  removed

Place the corn kernels in a medium bowl along with:
8 small cherry tomatoes, seeded, if
  desired, and halved
1 small ripe avocado, peeled and
  coarsely chopped
¼ cup coarsely chopped fresh basil
½ small red onion, finely diced, rinsed,
  and drained
2 tablespoons vegetable oil
2 tablespoons fresh lime juice, or
  to taste
1 clove garlic, finely chopped
1 to 3 fresh jalapeño peppers, seeded
  and finely chopped
Salt and ground black pepper to taste

Stir together well and serve immediately. This salsa will keep, covered and refrigerated, for 1 day.

Sloppy Joe

Sloppy Joe

The Sloppy Joe—known as loosemeat in certain parts of the country—dates from the 1950s. Why "Joe," it is not possible to say with certainty, but "sloppy" is obvious enough.

6 sandwiches

Heat in a large skillet, preferably non-stick, over medium heat:
>   1 tablespoon vegetable oil

Add:
>   1 small onion, finely diced
>   1 small red or yellow bell pepper, finely diced
>   4 cloves garlic, minced
>   1 large celery stalk, finely diced
>   1 teaspoon fresh thyme leaves (optional)
>   Salt and ground black pepper to taste

Cook, stirring frequently, until the onion is softened but not browned, about 10 minutes. Transfer the onion mixture to a plate. Add to the skillet and increase the heat slightly:
>   1¼ pounds ground beef chuck or sirloin

Cook, breaking up any lumps with a wooden spoon, just until browned, 3 to 4 minutes. Add the onion mixture along with:
>   ½ cup chili sauce
>   ½ cup beer or water
>   3 tablespoons Worcestershire sauce
>   Hot red pepper sauce to taste

Partially cover and simmer, stirring occasionally, until the flavors are blended and the sauce is slightly thickened, about 15 minutes. Toast, cut side up, under a broiler:
>   6 large seeded rolls or six 6-inch lengths French bread, halved

Sprinkle the Sloppy Joe mixture with:
>   3 tablespoons minced scallion greens

Spoon onto the bottom halves of the rolls and cover with the tops. Serve hot.

Oven-Roasted "French Fries"

Rutabagas and turnips also can be cooked this way.

4 servings

Preheat the oven to 450°F.

Peel and cut lengthwise into ⅜-inch-wide strips:
>   4 medium baking potatoes (about 1 pound)

Let soak in cold water for 10 minutes, then drain and dry well. Toss the potatoes with:
>   2 tablespoons vegetable or olive oil

Spread on a baking sheet and bake, turning several times, until golden, 30 to 40 minutes. Turn the potatoes onto paper towels to drain briefly, then sprinkle with:
>   ½ teaspoon salt
>   Paprika or ground black pepper to taste (optional)

Peanut Butter Cupcakes with Chocolate Frosting

Peanut Butter Cupcakes

Faster than lightning to make. Frost with Chocolate Satin Frosting, right.

18 cupcakes

Preheat the oven to 350°F. Line muffin pans with paper liners.

Combine in a food processor:
    1¼ **cups all-purpose flour**
    ¾ **cup packed light or dark brown sugar**
    1½ **teaspoons baking powder**
    ½ **teaspoon salt**
    ¾ **cup milk**
    ⅓ **cup creamy peanut butter**
    1 **large egg**
    1 **tablespoon unsalted butter, softened**
    1 **tablespoon vegetable oil**
    1 **teaspoon vanilla**
    ¾ **cup semisweet chocolate chips**

Pulse for a few seconds to mix. Scrape the sides of the bowl and the blade and pulse until smooth. Fill the muffin cups about two-thirds full. Bake until a toothpick inserted in the center of a cupcake comes out clean, 25 to 30 minutes. Remove from the pan and let cool completely on a rack before frosting.

Chocolate Satin Frosting

Kids and adults alike love this shiny dark sweet chocolate frosting, which is easily made in a food processor. Keep any extra in a jar in the refrigerator and melt it for a quick ice cream sauce, or spread it on graham crackers or cookies.

About 3 cups

Break or cut into 2 pieces:
    6 **ounces unsweetened chocolate**

Bring to a boil in a small saucepan:
    1 **cup evaporated milk or heavy cream**

Remove from the heat and add the chocolate pieces, without stirring. Cover and set aside for exactly 10 minutes. Scrape into a food processor or blender and add:
    1½ **cups sugar**
    6 **tablespoons (¾ stick) unsalted butter, cut into small pieces**
    1 **teaspoon vanilla**

Process until the mixture is perfectly smooth, 1 minute or more. Transfer to a bowl. If necessary, set aside for a few minutes (longer if you have used cream) until thickened to the desired spreading consistency. This keeps, refrigerated, for up to 1 week if made with cream, or about 3 weeks if made with evaporated milk. Or freeze for up to 6 months. Soften before using.

Tapioca Custard with Cocoa Whipped Cream

Tapioca Custard

Use the greater amount of tapioca if you like a thick pudding or if you are not adding egg.

4 to 6 servings

Whisk together thoroughly in a heavy saucepan:
**2½ cups whole or 2% low-fat milk
⅓ cup sugar
3 to 4 tablespoons quick-cooking
   tapioca
⅛ teaspoon salt**

Let stand for 10 minutes, then slowly bring to a simmer over medium heat, stirring constantly. Simmer, stirring, for 2 minutes. Gradually whisk about half of the pudding into:
1 or 2 large eggs, well beaten (optional)

Thoroughly stir this mixture into the remaining pudding. Cook, stirring, over low heat just until you see the first sign of thickening. Remove from the heat at once and stir in:
1 teaspoon vanilla

Let cool in the saucepan for 30 minutes; it will thicken considerably. Turn into cups or bowls. Serve warm or chilled. If you wish, accompany with:
Whipped cream, right

Whipped Cream

2 to 2½ cups

In a chilled bowl with chilled beaters, beat until thickened:
1 cup cold heavy cream

Add and beat to the desired consistency:
**2 teaspoons to 2 tablespoons sugar, 1 to
   4 tablespoons sifted powdered sugar,
   or 2 teaspoons honey (optional)
½ teaspoon vanilla (optional)**

Use immediately or see Holding Whipped Cream, right.

Cocoa Whipped Cream

Prepare Whipped Cream, above, combining a small amount of the cream and the vanilla with ⅓ cup sifted powdered sugar, 3 tablespoons unsweetened Dutch-process cocoa, and ⅛ teaspoon salt. Stir in the remaining cream and beat as directed, omitting the additional sugar.

HELPFUL HINT
Holding Whipped Cream

It is advisable to underwhip cream whenever it must be refrigerated for several hours before use. Whisk the cream briefly to the desired consistency just before use to reincorporate any liquid that may have separated from it.

Coffee Whipped Cream

Prepare Whipped Cream, left, adding 2 teaspoons instant coffee or espresso powder to the cream with the vanilla. Use about 1 tablespoon plus 2 teaspoons sugar, or to taste.

Mocha Whipped Cream

Prepare Whipped Cream, left, combining a small amount of the cream and the vanilla with 2 teaspoons instant coffee or espresso powder and 2 tablespoons unsweetened Dutch-process cocoa. Stir in the remaining cream and beat as directed, using 2 tablespoons sugar.

Winter Fruit Salad

Winter Fruit Salad

3 or 4 servings

Peel and section into a bowl, adding all
the juices:
  1 grapefruit
  1 orange

Refrigerate until cold. Not long before
serving, add:
  **1 apple, quartered, cored, and thinly
    sliced**
  1 banana, sliced

Stir to coat the flesh with citrus juice to
prevent discoloration. Stir in:
  **1 small bunch seedless red grapes,
    stemmed and halved**

Spoon the fruit salad into serving bowls.

Citrus Salad

6 servings

Grate 3 tablespoons zest from:
  4 navel oranges
  2 tangelos or 3 mandarins
  2 grapefruit

Peel and section the fruit and combine
with the zest and all the citrus juices.
Add:
  Sugar to taste (optional)
  2 tablespoons orange liqueur (optional)

Cover and refrigerate until ready to serve.

Broiled Grapefruit

*T*his delicious old-fashioned way with
*grapefruit can be served as a first course or
for dessert. Pink grapefruit is preferred for
its appealing color. These can be prepared
many hours in advance, then sugared and
broiled just before serving.*

4 servings

Adjust the broiler rack so that the
grapefruit will be about 4 inches below
a gas flame or 3 inches below an electric
element. Preheat the broiler.

Cut horizontally in half:
  2 grapefruit, preferably pink

Remove any large seeds. If desired, snip
out the tough centers. Loosen each section by cutting along the membranes
and skin with a small serrated knife or
grapefruit knife. Place the halves on a
small rimmed baking sheet. Sprinkle
with:
  1 tablespoon sugar
  **¼ teaspoon ground star anise or
    ground ginger (optional)**

Leaving the broiler door slightly ajar,
broil the grapefruit until the tops begin
to brown, about 5 minutes. Remove. For
garnish, place in the center of each half:
  1 small berry

Serve at once.

STEP-BY-STEP
*Peeling and Sectioning
Citrus Fruit*

Working on a grooved cutting board
to catch any juices, cut off the top
and bottom of the orange and
grapefruit.

Stand the fruit on the board and,
using a serrated knife, slice away the
rind from top to bottom. Trim away
any remaining white pith.

Working over a bowl, free each segment by cutting down against the
membrane on either side. Lift out
the segment and remove any seeds.

Peaches in Port and Madeleines

Peaches in Port

4 servings

Halve and remove the pits from:
2 ripe peaches

Cut each peach half into 4 slices. Place 4 slices in each of 4 stemmed glasses. Cover with:
Ruby port

Garnish with:
Fresh mint leaves

Madeleines

These buttery French teacakes, something between a sponge cake and a butter cake in texture, are traditionally baked in scallop-shaped madeleine molds, but you can use miniature muffin tins or small tartlet pans in any shape.

About 24 teacakes

Have all ingredients at room temperature, 68° to 70°F. Preheat the oven to 450°F. Using melted butter, generously grease 2 madeleine pans, each with 12 molds.

Sift together and return to the sifter:
1½ cups sifted cake flour
½ teaspoon baking powder
¼ teaspoon salt

In a medium bowl, mash and beat with a wooden spoon or rubber spatula until very soft and creamy:
12 tablespoons (1½ sticks) unsalted butter, cut into small pieces

If necessary, warm the bowl by dipping it into hot water to hasten the softening of the butter. In a large bowl, beat on high speed until thick and pale yellow, about 2 minutes:
3 large eggs
1 large egg yolk
¾ cup sugar
1½ teaspoons vanilla

Sift the flour mixture over the top of the egg mixture and fold in with a rubber spatula. Fold a dollop of the egg mixture into the butter. Scrape the butter mixture back into the remaining egg mixture and fold together. Let rest for at least 30 minutes.

Fill the molds three-quarters full; set any remaining batter aside. Bake until the cakes are golden on the top and golden brown around the edges, 8 to 10 minutes. Immediately loosen each cake with the tip of a slim knife and unmold onto a rack to cool. If necessary, wipe the molds clean, let cool, rebutter them, and repeat the baking process with the remaining batter. These are best the day they are made, but can be stored in an airtight container for a day or two.

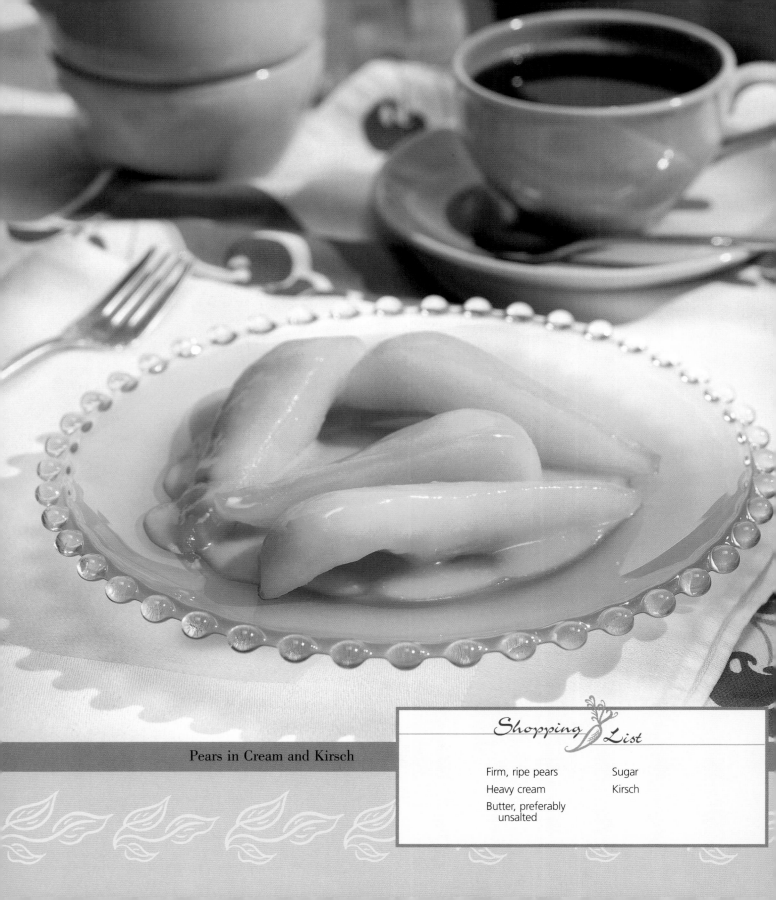

Pears in Cream and Kirsch

Firm, ripe pears	Sugar
Heavy cream	Kirsch
Butter, preferably unsalted	

Pears in Cream and Kirsch

Save this for those who appreciate understated elegance.

6 servings

Position a rack in the center of the oven. Preheat the oven to 425°F.

Peel, quarter lengthwise, and core:
**6 medium, firm ripe, sweet pears
(about 2½ pounds)**

Work quickly, and you will not need to worry that the flesh will darken—the pears will whiten in the kirsch. Melt over medium heat in your largest skillet, one in which the pears will just fit in a single layer:
2 tablespoons butter, preferably unsalted

Add the pears and sprinkle over:
**3 tablespoons sugar
¼ cup kirsch**

Cook over medium-low heat, turning the pears frequently with a wooden spoon, until they are tender when tested with a thin skewer, 5 to 20 minutes, depending on the ripeness of the pears. Arrange the pears, cut sides down, in a 9 x 9-inch baking dish. Add to the skillet:
¼ cup heavy cream

Boil this sauce over high heat until slightly thickened, 30 seconds to 2 minutes, then pour over the pears. Bake just until the cream on top sets into a skin, about 10 minutes. Serve at once. The dish will look plain but needs no garnish.

Bananas Foster

This classic recipe is from Brennan's restaurant in New Orleans.

4 servings

Peel and cut in half lengthwise:
4 firm ripe bananas

Cut each length into 4 pieces. In a large, heavy skillet, melt:
2 tablespoons butter

Place the bananas in the skillet cut sides down. Cook over low heat for 5 minutes, then turn with a spatula and cook for another 5 minutes, just until fork-tender—do not overcook. Sprinkle with:
**3 tablespoons light brown sugar
¼ teaspoon ground cinnamon
⅛ teaspoon ground nutmeg**

Transfer the bananas to a heatproof serving dish and arrange in a single layer. Add to the skillet:
**½ cup dark rum
1 tablespoon brandy (optional)**

Over medium heat, use a spatula to loosen caramelized bits while the spirits heat. When the tip of a finger tells you they are hot, ignite with a long wooden match, then pour over the bananas. Spoon over:
Vanilla ice cream

Buttered Apple Slices

4 servings

Melt in a large skillet over medium-low heat until foamy:
2 tablespoons butter

Add in a single layer:
**2 firm, tart apples, cored and cut into
⅜-inch slices**

Cook until the bottoms are golden. Turn and cook the second side until golden, a few minutes longer, depending on the firmness of the apples. Do not let them turn soft.

To glaze, especially if they are very tart, sprinkle over the surface:
2 tablespoons sugar

Let stand until the sugar melts.

Serve warm.

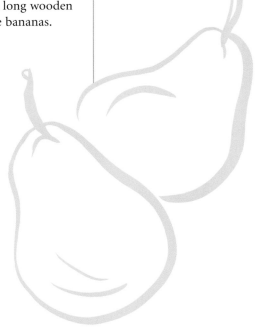

Pineapple in Hot Buttered Rum Sauce

Shopping List

Pineapple

Butter, preferably
    unsalted

Dark brown sugar

Dark rum

Ground allspice

Macaroons or
    unsweetened
    shredded coconut

Pineapple in Hot Buttered Rum Sauce

4 servings

Combine in a wide, nonreactive skillet:
   4 tablespoons (½ stick) unsalted butter
   ¼ cup packed dark brown sugar
   ¼ cup dark rum
   ½ teaspoon ground allspice

Heat, stirring, over low heat until the sugar is dissolved and the syrup is thick and bubbly. Add:
   1 large ripe pineapple, peeled, cored, and cut into bite-sized chunks, with juices

Heat, basting the pineapple with the syrup, until it is heated through. Divide the pineapple among 4 serving bowls, spoon the sauce over, and sprinkle with:
   Crushed macaroon crumbs or unsweetened shredded coconut, lightly toasted

Serve immediately.

Glazed Pineapple Rings

8 to 10 rings

Preheat the broiler. Butter a broiling pan.

Trim, peel, and cut crosswise into ½-inch-thick slices:
   1 large ripe pineapple

Using an apple corer, a small cookie cutter, or a sharp knife, cut out the core in each ring. Arrange the rings on the buttered pan and drizzle with:
   4 to 5 tablespoons melted butter

Sprinkle the rings with:
   About ½ cup sugar

Broil, without turning, until hot and golden, 5 to 8 minutes. Serve hot.

STEP-BY-STEP
Chunking a Pineapple

Using a large, heavy knife, cut off the leaves at their base and a slice off the bottom. Stand up the pineapple and slice away the rind.

Using the same knife, cut the pineapple lengthwise into quarters.

Cut the hard triangular core of the pineapple away from the flesh of each quarter and discard it.

Cut the quarters into bite-sized chunks, adding the juices to the bowl with the chunks.

Summer Fruit Cup

Shopping List

Cantaloupe

Sweet cherries

Raspberries, blackberries, or blueberries

Fresh mint

Orange juice

Crème de cassis or orange liqueur

Summer Fruit Cup

2 servings

Halve and seed:
1 perfectly ripe small cantaloupe

Using the small end of a melon baller, make round balls of the cantaloupe by pressing the baller deep into the flesh until juice comes out of the hole in the bottom of the baller, twisting to cut a whole ball, and removing. Combine the melon balls with:
½ cup fresh sweet cherries, pitted
1 tablespoon orange juice
1 tablespoon crème de cassis or orange liqueur

Scoop out the remaining craters of flesh from the cantaloupe halves to make a smooth container (save the flesh for another use). Just before serving, gently toss the melon mixture with:
½ cup fresh raspberries, blackberries, or blueberries

Divide the fruit between the melon shells. Garnish with:
Fresh mint sprigs

Melon with Port

4 servings

Cut a thin slice from both stem and blossom end of:
2 perfectly ripe small cantaloupes or other dessert melons

Cut the melons horizontally in half, scoop out the seeds, place on individual serving plates, and pour into each half:
Up to ¼ cup ruby port

Cover loosely with plastic wrap and let stand at room temperature for 30 minutes before serving.

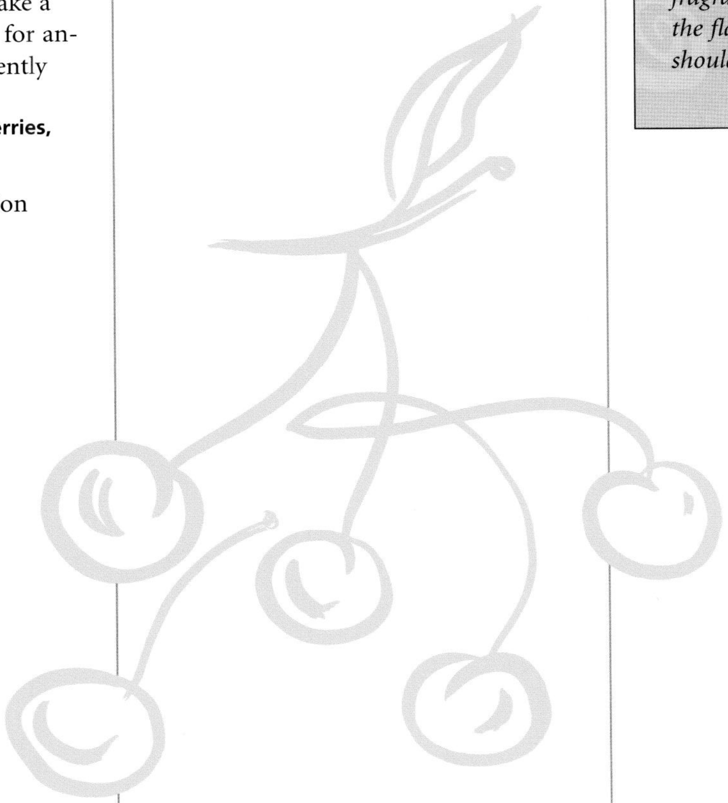

KITCHEN TIP
Cantaloupe

If a melon has no fruity perfume at the smooth (the blossom) end, do not buy it. There also should be a slight softness at the blossom end. Choose melons that are heaviest for their size, with no soft spots, mold, or cracks and no strong aroma indicating over-ripeness. If, when you gently shake a melon, seeds rattle, chances are the melon is too ripe.

Choose cantaloupe in which the netting is pronounced and the fragrance is as sweet as you expect the flavor to be. The melon's flesh should be musky and orange.

Pantry

A few simple preparations can make quick meals even more appealing to you, your family, and your guests. Classic sauces such as vinaigrette or mayonnaise, easy to make with a blender or food processor, enrich salads and fish. Flavored butters add savory elegance to grilled meats and fish—make them ahead and freeze them. Salsas perk up meat dishes as well as vegetables. A raw tomato sauce captures the essence of fresh tomatoes; warm it by tossing it with hot pasta. The Pantry offers several ways to cook rice in less time than it takes to prepare many main courses—30 minutes from start to finish. With the following basic recipes in your repertoire you can put your personal mark on a quick weeknight meal.

Vinaigrette

MAKING A VINAIGRETTE

The surefire way to make a thick, well-emulsified vinaigrette is to first whisk together the vinegar or lemon juice and the seasonings (salt, minced shallots or other members of the onion tribe, and mustard) in a small bowl. Then slowly add the oil, drop by drop, whisking as you go, until the dressing begins to thicken. Add the oil in more of a steady stream as the dressing becomes noticeably thicker. An alternative, and perhaps more convenient, technique is to place the vinegar or lemon juice and seasonings in a small jar with a tight-fitting lid and shake to blend. Then add the oil in three or four additions, shaking vigorously between additions. A third and equally popular method is to mix the vinegar and seasonings in a blender and then add the oil in a slow, steady stream with the machine running. Vinaigrette can be stored, tightly covered, in the refrigerator for up to two weeks.

From left, Reduced-Fat Vinaigrette, Fresh Herb Vinaigrette, French Dressing

Basic Vinaigrette or French Dressing

Vinaigrette is the preferred dressing in France for green salads, avocados, artichokes, and many kinds of sliced, shredded, or chopped vegetables. It is also the starting point for a host of more complicated dressings and accepts a variety of accents with additional ingredients. The optional ingredients in this recipe not only add flavor but also help maintain the emulsion of oil and vinegar that is essential to a good vinaigrette.

About 1½ cups

If a garlic flavor is desired, mash together until a paste is formed:
- **1 small clove garlic, peeled**
- **2 to 3 pinches of salt**

Remove to a small bowl or a jar with a tight-fitting lid. Add and whisk or shake until well blended:
- **⅓ to ½ cup red wine vinegar or fresh lemon juice**
- **1 shallot, minced**
- **1 teaspoon Dijon mustard (optional)**
- **Salt and ground black pepper to taste**

Add in a slow, steady stream, whisking constantly, or add to the jar and shake until smooth:
- **1 cup extra-virgin olive oil**

Taste and adjust the seasonings. Use at once or cover and refrigerate.

Reduced-Fat Vinaigrette

This recipe uses chicken stock to replace much of the oil. While this dressing will never be as emulsified as a standard vinaigrette, it is much lower in calories. Use only fresh, flavorful stock.

About 1½ cups

Whisk together in a small bowl or shake in a jar with a tight-fitting lid:
- **3 tablespoons red wine vinegar or fresh lemon juice**
- **1 tablespoon Dijon mustard**
- **1 clove garlic, minced**
- **Salt and ground black pepper to taste**

Add in a slow, steady stream, whisking constantly, or add to the jar and shake until smooth:
- **¾ cup chicken stock**
- **3 tablespoons extra-virgin olive oil**

Taste and adjust the seasonings. Use at once or cover and refrigerate.

Fresh Herb Vinaigrette

Prepare Basic Vinaigrette, left, or Reduced-Fat Vinaigrette, above, adding ⅓ cup minced or finely snipped fresh herbs (basil, dill, parsley, chives, and/or thyme).

Mayonnaise

WHIPPING UP HOMEMADE MAYONNAISE

If you are accustomed to store-bought mayonnaise, your first taste of homemade will be a surprise. Homemade mayonnaise is an elegant French sauce, not a sandwich spread (although you can make it thick enough to spread). The flavor is bright with lemon juice or vinegar and nutty with good oil. Homemade mayonnaise is sumptuous and can be made quickly.

Making the sauce in a food processor or blender or with an electric mixer is practically foolproof, and the sauce has greater volume and a fluffier texture than when made by hand. For the finest and silkiest texture of all, make the sauce by hand. Remember that ingredients at room temperature emulsify more readily than cold ones.

Homemade mayonnaise can be kept, tightly covered in the refrigerator, for a day or two, but it will lose some of its sheen after a few hours. The maximum time mayonnaise should be out of the refrigerator is 2 hours—and when the air temperature is 85°F or above, it is 1 hour.

To perk up store-bought mayonnaise for a sauce in a pinch, fold in an equal amount of sour cream or beat an equal amount of chilled heavy cream and fold it in.

Traditional Mayonnaise

This is our basic mayonnaise, from which all of our variations can be prepared. It can be whisked to a lighter consistency by gradually adding an appropriately flavored stock, vegetable juice, or even spirits. Use a ceramic, glass, or stainless-steel bowl—aluminum or copper will react with the acid and affect the color and even the flavor of the sauce.

About 1 cup

Whisk together in a medium bowl until smooth and light:

2 large egg yolks
1 to 2 tablespoons fresh lemon juice or white wine vinegar
¼ teaspoon salt
Pinch of ground white pepper

Whisk in by drops until the mixture starts to thicken and stiffen:

1 cup vegetable oil, at room temperature

As the sauce begins to thicken—when about one-third has been added—whisk in the oil more steadily, making sure each addition is thoroughly blended before adding the next. Should the oil stop being absorbed, whisk vigorously before adding more. Stir in:

Up to 1½ teaspoons Dijon mustard (optional)
Salt and ground black pepper to taste

Serve immediately or refrigerate in a covered jar for 1 to 2 days.

Blender Mayonnaise

If using a food processor, use the plastic blade if you have one, as it seems to make a slightly lighter sauce. Egg white is needed in machine-made mayonnaise. Beat 1 egg well with a fork to blend the yolk and white, let it settle a few seconds, then measure. This recipe can be doubled, in which case, just use 1 large egg.

About 1 cup

Combine in a blender or food processor:

2 tablespoons well-beaten egg
1 large egg yolk
¼ teaspoon dry or Dijon mustard

Process on high speed until well blended, about 5 seconds in a blender, 15 seconds in a food processor fitted with the plastic blade, 30 seconds in a food processor fitted with the steel blade. Scrape down the sides, then sprinkle the mixture with:

1 teaspoon fresh lemon juice and/or white wine vinegar or rice vinegar
¼ teaspoon salt

Process for about 2 minutes in a blender, 15 seconds in a food processor fitted with the plastic blade, 7 to 8 seconds in a food processor fitted with the steel blade. Have ready in a small spouted measuring pitcher:

¾ cup vegetable oil, at room temperature

With the machine running, add the oil in the thinnest possible stream. After about one-third of the oil has been added—the mixture will have swollen and stiffened—add the oil in a slightly thicker stream. Stop the machine when all has been added and scrape down the sides and around the blade, mixing in any unabsorbed oil. If you want a thicker sauce, add as before:

Up to ¼ cup vegetable oil, at room temperature

Should the sauce be too thick, add as needed:

Light or heavy cream, milk, or water, at room temperature

Taste the mayonnaise and stir in:

1½ to 3 teaspoons fresh lemon juice or white wine vinegar
½ to 1 teaspoon dry or Dijon mustard
Salt and ground white pepper to taste

Serve immediately, or refrigerate in a covered jar for 1 to 2 days.

Eggs for mayonnaise

Curry Mayonnaise

Superb with cold vegetables, eggs, fish, poultry, and meats (everything!).

Prepare Traditional Mayonnaise, opposite, or Blender Mayonnaise, opposite, and set aside. In a small skillet, stir 2 tablespoons best-quality curry powder into 2 tablespoons mild-tasting oil, such as olive or vegetable oil, over low heat for 30 to 60 seconds—until you start to smell it. Let cool and whisk into the mayonnaise. Season to taste with salt and ground black pepper.

Tartar Sauce

Prepare Traditional Mayonnaise, opposite, or Blender Mayonnaise, opposite, and stir in 1 tablespoon minced scallions (or onions or shallots), 1½ teaspoons minced sour gherkins or dill pickles, 1½ teaspoons drained capers, and 1½ teaspoons drained sweet pickle relish or minced sweet pickles, if desired. Heighten the flavors with a dash or two of fresh lemon juice or hot red pepper sauce. Serve sprinkled with 1 tablespoon minced fresh parsley and 1 tablespoon finely snipped fresh chives.

Garlic Mayonnaise (Aïoli)

Sometimes called beurre de Provence—the butter of Provence—aïoli is traditionally served slightly chilled as a sauce for cold poached fish, vegetables, meat, or eggs. It also makes a luxurious garnish for hot and cold soups. Aïoli is a contraction of the Provençal words for garlic and oil.

About 1 cup

Whisk together in a medium bowl until smooth and light:

2 large egg yolks
4 to 6 cloves garlic, finely minced
Salt and ground white pepper to taste

Whisk in by drops until the mixture starts to thicken and stiffen:

1 cup olive oil, or part olive and part saf-
flower or peanut oil, at room temperature

As the sauce begins to thicken, whisk in the oil more steadily, making sure each addition is thoroughly blended before adding the next. Gradually whisk in:

1 teaspoon fresh lemon juice, or to taste
½ teaspoon cold water

Taste and adjust the seasonings.

Serve immediately or refrigerate in a jar for 1 to 2 days.

EGG SAFETY

The best eggs are the freshest ones. The shell naturally protects an egg, and if it is cracked or damaged, the contents will deteriorate rapidly; eggs with cracked, damaged, or dirty shells should not be used.

The bacteria Salmonella enteritidis, which can cause illness and even death, are occasionally found in raw eggs, even uncracked eggs. While the risk remains extremely low (it is estimated that 1 in 10,000 eggs is infected), we recommend handling eggs carefully, particularly when cooking for young children, the elderly, pregnant women, or anyone with a compromised immune system. Buy refrigerated eggs and get them to your own refrigerator as quickly as possible. Never use a doubtful egg. When cracking or separating eggs, make sure that the fresh egg never touches the exterior of the shell, which is more apt to carry contamination. Before and after handling eggs, wash your hands and any utensils or equipment that may come into contact with either the shell or the contents.

Of great concern to some are a number of classic recipes that depend on raw eggs—among them mayonnaise. Some cooks now substitute pasteurized liquid eggs (available both whole and separated into yolks and whites). The liquid eggs closely resemble fresh eggs and are only slightly less efficient than fresh eggs for emulsifying or whipping purposes. Some cooks refuse to compromise and continue using fresh eggs. If you are of this school, minimize risk by using the freshest eggs possible and storing them at temperatures below 40°F.

Flavored Butter (Beurre Composé)

BLENDING A FLAVORED BUTTER

Made by blending herbs or other flavorings into plain butter, these are versatile, quick to make, and easy to store. Flavored butters are served either cold or at room temperature, as decorative garnishes or as instant sauces. Uncooked flavored butters are simply softened butter mixed with spices, herbs, or other pureed or chopped ingredients. The butter can be used immediately while still soft, or rolled into cylinders in pieces of wax or parchment paper, plastic wrap, or aluminum foil, then refrigerated for 1½ to 2 hours, or frozen, and sliced into thin rounds to garnish dishes just before serving. Allow about 1 tablespoon per serving. (Flavored butters can be frozen for several weeks, but they should not be refrigerated for more than 24 hours.) Start with fresh butter of the highest quality, preferably unsalted.

For guests, we smooth the butter into a small bowl in which it just fits and run a fork over the top in a decorative swirl or crosshatch. The butter is served at room temperature with a butter knife.

Basic Flavored Butter

About ¼ cup

In a small bowl, cream with a fork or wooden spoon:

4 tablespoons (½ stick) butter (preferably unsalted), softened

Gradually stir in flavorings as desired along with:

Salt and ground white pepper to taste

Roll the mixture into a cylinder in a piece of wax or parchment paper, plastic wrap, or aluminum foil (or shape as desired) and refrigerate or freeze until firm enough to slice. Or refrigerate in a small bowl or ramekin and spoon on just before serving.

Soy Sauce Butter

For grilled fish, chicken, and beef, especially in an Asian-style menu.

Prepare Basic Flavored Butter, above, and whisk in 2 to 3 teaspoons soy sauce.

Maître d'Hôtel Butter (Lemon and Parsley)

Traditionally served over broiled steak.

Prepare Basic Flavored Butter, left, and add 1 tablespoon finely chopped parsley and ¾ to 1½ tablespoons fresh lemon juice.

Anchovy Butter

For broiled fish, steak, and lamb chops and as a canapé spread.

Prepare Basic Flavored Butter, left, and add 1 teaspoon anchovy paste, ¼ teaspoon fresh lemon juice, or to taste, and salt and ground red pepper to taste.

From left, Anchovy Butter, Basic Flavored Butter, Maître d'Hôtel Butter, Soy Sauce Butter

Rice

RICE BASICS

A cook needs to know two things about rice. The first is whether the bran and germ are still attached. If so, it is brown rice (although in some cases, such as Thai black rice, the rice is another color). The advantages of brown rice are its much higher fiber content and the presence of vitamins and minerals that are lost in white rice. The disadvantages are its longer cooking time and its perishability: Brown rice must be refrigerated and used within a month. White rice offers two advantages: year-long shelf life and relatively quick cooking.

If rice is parboiled before the bran is removed, it retains more B vitamins. The resulting white rice is known as "converted" and takes a little more liquid and a little longer to cook than other white rice but shares the same shelf life. If rice is cooked and dried again before packaging, it becomes "instant," a less flavorful product with softer kernels but a convenience nevertheless, especially with brown rice.

The second thing is the length of the grain. A kernel of long-grain rice, brown or white, is three to five times longer than it is wide; the cooked kernels are fluffy and separate easily. Medium- and short-grain rice kernels are closer to oval in shape, less than twice as long as they are wide, and contain more amylopectin, a waxy starch molecule that makes the cooked rice denser and the kernels more apt to cohere. Medium- and short-grain rice, if steamed or simmered the same way as long-grain rice, need about ¼ to ½ cup less water per cup of rice and thus a few minutes less cooking time.

Clockwise from left, brown rice, medium-grain white rice, long-grain white rice

Basic Cooked White Rice

Use 2 cups water for soft, tender rice or 1¾ to 1⅞ cups for firmer grains. Use ¼ cup less, either way, when cooking medium-grain white rice. Do not stir, except as directed, or the rice will turn gummy.

3 cups; 4 servings

I. Bring to a boil in a medium saucepan:
   1¾ to 2 cups water
   1 tablespoon butter or vegetable oil (optional)
   ¼ to ½ teaspoon salt

Add and stir once:
   1 cup long-grain white rice

Cover and cook over very low heat until all the water is absorbed, 15 to 18 minutes. Do not lift the cover before the end of cooking. Let stand, covered, for 5 to 10 minutes before serving.

II. This method is popular in the American South, Latin America, and parts of Europe.

Spread in a large, broad, shallow, heavy saucepan to a depth of only 2 or 3 grains:
   1 cup long-grain or medium-grain white rice

Add just enough liquid to cover the rice by ½ inch or the thickness of your hand. Bring to a gentle boil and stir once. Cook, uncovered, over low heat until the liquid is almost absorbed, about 5 minutes. Cover the saucepan and continue to cook for 15 to 18 minutes. Do not lift the cover before the end of cooking. Let stand, covered, for 5 to 10 minutes before serving.

Oven-Baked White Rice

This foolproof rice goes well with roasted chicken or broiled or baked fish.

4 servings

Preheat the oven to 350°F.

Melt or heat in a 2-quart stovetop-to-oven casserole over medium heat:
   1 tablespoon butter or olive oil

Add and cook, stirring, until softened, 3 to 5 minutes:
   ½ cup chopped onions

Add and stir until well coated:
   1 cup long-grain white rice

Add:
   2 cups chicken stock
   ¼ teaspoon salt

Bring to a boil. Cover and bake until the rice is tender and the stock is absorbed, 20 to 25 minutes. Let stand, covered, for 5 minutes before serving.

Salsa Fresca, left, Salsa Verde, right

Basic Pilaf

Rice stirred in hot butter or oil before simmering is very flavorful and fluffy, especially if you use basmati rice. The preparation is known as a pilaf, and it traditionally calls for seasonings to be sautéed in the pot with the rice. The name can be traced to the Persian pilau. All kinds of variations are found in the Middle East, the Caucasus, and India.

4 servings

Melt in a large saucepan or deep skillet over low heat:

   2 tablespoons butter

Add and cook, stirring, until golden, about 8 minutes:

   ½ cup chopped onions

Add and cook, stirring, until coated, about 3 minutes:

   1 cup white basmati rice

Stir in:

   2 cups water or chicken stock
   ½ teaspoon salt (if using water)

Bring to a boil. Stir once, cover, and cook over low heat until the liquid is absorbed and the rice is tender, about 15 minutes. Do not stir. Let stand, covered, for 5 minutes before serving. Sprinkle with:

   2 tablespoons chopped walnuts, toasted, or
   2 tablespoons chopped fresh parsley

Basic Cooked Brown Rice

Use 2¼ to 2½ cups water for long-grain brown rice or 2 to 2¼ cups water for short-grain brown rice; the larger amount yields softer, slightly stickier rice. Short-grain brown rice cooks a little faster than long-grain. Do not stir except as directed.

3½ cups; 4 servings

Bring to a boil in a medium saucepan:

   2 to 2½ cups water
   1 tablespoon butter (optional)
   ¼ to ½ teaspoon salt

Add and stir once:

   1 cup brown rice

Cover and cook over very low heat until all the water is absorbed, 35 to 45 minutes. Do not lift the cover before the end of cooking. Let stand, covered, for 5 to 10 minutes before serving.

Sauce & Salsa

Fresh Tomato Sauce

Summer's best. Make this easy sauce when you can get juicy, ripe tomatoes.

Enough for 1 pound pasta

Drain in a colander for 20 minutes:

5 large ripe tomatoes, seeded and finely diced

Remove to a large bowl and stir in:

½ cup fresh basil leaves, finely chopped

3 tablespoons olive oil

2 cloves garlic, finely minced

Salt and ground black pepper to taste

Let stand for at least 30 minutes. Serve the sauce at room temperature. If serving over hot pasta, sprinkle each portion with:

1 to 2 teaspoons balsamic vinegar

Ripe tomatoes, fresh basil, and garlic for Fresh Tomato Sauce

Salsa Fresca

This recipe for Mexican salsa is easily doubled or tripled, but try to make only as much as you will use immediately, as it loses its texture on standing and the chili peppers increase in heat. Regional variations use scallions or white or red onions, water instead of lime juice, and in Yucatán, sour-orange juice instead of lime juice. Any sort of fresh chili pepper can be used—each contributes its distinctive character. Rinsing the chopped onions eliminates the biting aftertaste that could otherwise overwhelm the other ingredients. As you can see, precise amounts are less important than the happy marriage of flavors, so taste as you go. Salsa Fresca complements everything from tacos to hot grills to cool vegetables. In American-style Mexican food, this type of salsa is sometimes called pico de gallo.

About 2 cups

Combine in a medium bowl:

½ small white or red onion or 8 slender scallions, finely chopped, rinsed, and drained

2 tablespoons fresh lime juice or cold water

Prepare the following ingredients, setting them aside, then add all together to the onion mixture:

2 large ripe tomatoes, or 3 to 5 ripe plum tomatoes, seeded, if desired, and finely diced

¼ to ½ cup chopped fresh cilantro (leaves and tender stems)

3 to 5 serrano or fresh jalapeño peppers, or ¼ to 1 habanero pepper, or to taste, seeded and minced

6 radishes, finely diced (optional)

1 medium clove garlic, minced (optional)

Stir together well. Season with:

¼ teaspoon salt, or to taste

Serve immediately.

Salsa Verde

This classic Italian tart green sauce is traditionally served with braised meats, fried calamari, and grilled fish dishes.

About 1 cup

Place in a food processor:

⅔ cup parsley leaves

2½ tablespoons drained capers

6 anchovy fillets (optional)

½ teaspoon finely chopped garlic

½ teaspoon Dijon mustard

½ teaspoon red wine vinegar or 1 tablespoon freshly squeezed lemon juice

½ cup olive oil

Salt to taste

Blend to a uniform consistency, but do not overprocess. Adjust the seasonings. Serve at room temperature or store, covered and refrigerated, for up to 1 week.

Index

*Numerals in italics indicate an illustration
of the subject mentioned.*

Acknowledgments

The following kindly lent props for photography:
Amano, Washington, D.C.; Appalachian Spring,
Washington, D.C.; April Cornell, Washington,
D.C.; Corso de' Fiori, Washington, D.C.; Crate & Barrel,
Washington, D.C.; French Country Living Store, Great
Falls, Virginia; Ginza, Washington, D.C.; Grapevine
Consignment and Antiques, Bethesda, Maryland; The
Kitchen Store, Washington, D.C.; Marcella Kogan,
Wheaton, Maryland; Michael Round Fine China and
Crystal, Bethesda, Maryland; Nimmi Damodaran,
Washington, D.C.; Pine Grove Antiques, Phillipsport,
New York; Sam & Harry's, Washington, D.C.; Santa Fe
Style, Washington, D.C.; Tiny Jewel Box, Washington,
D.C.; Williams-Sonoma, Washington, D.C.

The editors wish to thank the following individuals for
their valuable assistance: Heather Allen, Washington,
D.C.; Ellen Callaway, Triangle, Virginia; Darren Smith,
Washington, D.C.